Sensual Secrets

SENSUAL SECRETS

How to be Lucky in Love

RODNEY DAVIES

*who was born on 14 February,
St Valentines Day*

Aquarian/Thorsons
An Imprint of HarperCollins*Publishers*

The Aquarian Press
An Imprint of HarperCollins*Publishers*
77–85 Fulham Palace Road,
Hammersmith, London W6 8JB

Published by The Aquarian Press 1992
1 3 5 7 9 10 8 6 4 2

A catalogue record for this book
is available from the British Library

ISBN 1 85538 170 2

Printed in Great Britain by
HarperCollinsManufacturing Glasgow

CONTENTS

INTRODUCTION

Love, as the old saying tells us, makes the world go round. Love draws us together, love makes us feel special, love stimulates creativity and motivates men and women to achieve far more than they ever thought possible. Love is a catalyst, which brings out the best in us all, while at the same time satisfying our yearning to be loved in return. And this is why love is regarded as the ideal emotional state that enables a man and a woman to cleave to each other until death do them part.

This book is about romantic love – that elusive madness which disrupts all normal patterns of thought and feeling – and how you, the reader, can attract it.

Because love often strikes when least expected, it has been personified since ancient times as Eros or Cupid, an irresponsible and naughty child who shoots his deadly arrows into our hearts at random. Sometimes he behaves cruelly, firing an arrow into one person's heart but not into the heart of the other. Or he may cause mischief by making us fall in love when we are quite unsuited to one another. Yet he also, in fairness, sometimes gets it right, thus bringing two people together in the most sublime relationship known to man.

But whether or not you believe in Cupid, it *is* possible to increase your chances of meeting someone and falling in love. If you follow the advice in *Sensual Secrets* it may not be long before you too are gripped by that 'divine madness' and have found a lover who's just as crazy about you.

Before you set off on this wonderful journey, remember that the road ahead may be pleasant and flower-bordered in places but it will be rocky and hazardous in others. And this is perhaps how it should be, for without love's uncertainties to provide a contrast, we might not experience the glory and rapture that are its true delights.

And be prepared – for Cupid may be looking in your direction and taking an arrow from his quiver right now!

Chapter 1
LOVE IN THE STARS

Astrology can tell you a lot about your romantic nature. It gives you a better understanding of yourself and helps you identify the most compatible partner.

This ancient art originated about 3,500 years ago in the Middle East where the first astrologers thought the planets were divine and had the power to control what went on down here on Earth. Modern astrologers no longer think the planets are divine, though they still believe our lives are influenced by them. I think they are best regarded as symbols of ourselves, representing our appearance, our health, our personality and our fate.

At the moment you are born, the positions of the planets in the sky mirror all that you are and all that you will become. And when an astrologer is given the time, date and place of your birth, he or she can draw up an astrological chart which plots the planetary positions at that moment in the encircling starry constellations or zodiac signs.

A good deal of information can be gained from the position of the sun in the zodiac on your birthday (your sun sign), and also from the zodiac sign which was rising above the horizon (your rising sign).

SUN SIGNS

Most people nowadays know their birth sign or sun sign, but if you are uncertain of yours you can easily find it out from the list below:

Born between	*Sun sign*
21 March–20 April	Aries, the Ram
21 April–21 May	Taurus, the Bull
22 May–21 June	Gemini, the Twins
22 June–23 July	Cancer, the Crab
24 July–23 August	Leo, the Lion
24 August–23 September	Virgo, the Virgin
24 September–22 October	Libra, the Scales
23 October–22 November	Scorpio, the Scorpion
23 November–22 December	Sagittarius, the Centaur
23 December–20 January	Capricorn, the Goat
21 January–19 February	Aquarius, the Water-Pourer
20 February–20 March	Pisces, the Fish

The twelve zodiac signs are arranged in four groups, each group being linked with one of the ancient elements – Fire, Air, Earth and Water. Aries, Leo and Sagittarius are Fire signs; Gemini, Libra and Aquarius are Air signs; Taurus, Virgo and Capricorn are Earth signs; and Cancer, Scorpio and Pisces are Water signs.

The sun symbolizes the ego or conscious mind. So those born with the sun in one or other of the Fire signs tend to have lots of energy, confidence and enthusiasm; if the sun was in an Air sign, the person is usually distinguished by his or her independence, intelligence and creativity; if the sun was in an Earth sign, the character is typically conservative, stubborn and practical; while if the Sun was in a Water sign, the person tends to be adaptable, sensitive and sympathetic.

These and your other sun-sign traits affect your talent for lovemaking and determine the importance of romance in your life. What then does your sun sign say about you as a person? And more particularly, what does it say about you and love? The following character sketches may help to answer these questions.

Aries, the Ram

You may not be very tall but you are strong and usually hard-working. You are also blessed with an outgoing, enthusiastic and ambitious nature, which – together with your considerable energy – makes you a natural leader. You prefer giving orders to taking them, and you tend to be brave and adventurous. But you lack staying power. If you launch a new project you try to get others to take care of the boring, day-to-day details while you race off to seek a fresh challenge.

You are basically extroverted and sociable but also somewhat insecure. You often lack confidence in your personal attractiveness. If you're a man you may worry about being small. If you're a woman you might be anxious about your small breasts or plump thighs. Arians also tend to be very hairy, though this is obviously less of a problem for Aries men.

Your feelings about your own appearance may prompt you to associate with those who are less attractive than you, or who have certain character flaws. Your insecurity sometimes creates jealousy and uncertainty in your love relationships; and because you are hot-tempered, your romantic involvements tend to be stormy.

Both male and female Arians have a strong sex drive. This is no bad thing in itself but it could mean that you get into sexual relationships rather too easily and frequently. With the right partner, you are an ardent and sensual lover.

Your love affairs are very important to you, chiefly because you hate being alone, but also because you need the ego boost of having someone lose their heart to you. You are at your best in the early stages of a love affair, when your generosity, good humour and fun-loving nature come to the fore. But as time goes by your enthusiasm wears off and your charm may turn into irritability, suspicion and bad temper. In love, as in work, you are unsuited to the long haul. Bear in mind that if you

keep changing partners so frequently, you may never find
the romantic bliss you seek.
Romance rating: 6

Taurus, the Bull
Like the Arian, you usually have a stocky, strong
physique. You are both practical and artistic, qualities
which can make you a skilled craftsman or a talented
potter, sculptor or painter. You are also blessed with a
pleasant singing voice and a good ear for music. Perhaps
you play a musical instrument or even make your living
as a musician?

You are friendly and enjoy having a laugh, qualities
that make you the most sociable of the Earth sign types.
Yet, again like the Arian, you are somewhat insecure,
which may mean that you underestimate your attractiveness. This is why you frequently exploit your musical
or other artistic talents as a way of meeting and appealing
to the opposite sex.

You are essentially a stable, conservative and rather
stubborn person, who likes to know where you are going.
Financial security is important to you, as is your home
life, which means that you seldom take risks or gamble.
You are probably looking forward to the day when you
get married, as this will give you a sense of security which
might otherwise be lacking in your life. With this in
mind, you tend to examine your lovers with a fairly
critical eye to make sure that they have the right qualities
for a long-term partner.

Your strong sex drive may lead you to play the field
when you are young, and perhaps even later on, when
you have supposedly settled down. You like comfort,
eating and material possessions. Indeed, your homemak-
ing and cooking talents, combined with your ardent
nature, make you an excellent partner.

Yet because you tend to prefer the familiar, and to have
little interest in either ideas or the world around you, you
may soon bore those who are more outgoing and intellec-

tual. This is less of a problem for those Taurus women who choose to focus their attention on their home and children but it may cause difficulties for the Taurus man if he marries a woman who thrives on change and adventure.
Romance rating: 3

Gemini, the Twins
You probably have an attractive face and body, an engaging manner and a bright smile, which attract others to you like bees to honey. This is why you seldom want for friends or would-be lovers, even though lovemaking as such is not that high on your list of priorities. You are also fortunate in having a clear, smooth complexion, which makes you look much younger than you are. And your natural slimness means that you don't have to spend time dieting or worrying about what you eat.

You probably also have a quick, intelligent mind, a good memory and a clever way with words, which helps make you an amusing and interesting companion. This is why you are drawn to those jobs – like selling – that entail persuading and influencing others. Yet, while you may be well-read, you lack the stamina to become a specialist – your knowledge tends to be wide but not very deep.

Where the opposite sex is concerned, you prefer those who have minds of their own and who like to talk, and you will choose brains over beauty any day. The Gemini woman may find that she often attracts men who are her intellectual inferiors. In the short term she enjoys running mental rings around them but in the long term she will find them dull.

Geminians have a dislike of emotional display, which they regard as both childish and unnecessary. This is why you may have difficulty falling in love – being in love would give the person concerned too much power over you. Your ideal relationship is one where there is a meeting of minds, not of hearts.

You are not very interested in lovemaking, which you

may regard as an unappealing, even slightly disgusting, activity. You will have discovered sex quite early, though your sexual adventures are prompted more by curiosity than by passion. You are not a very enthusiastic lover, especially as you have trouble in becoming emotionally involved with your partners in the first place. Geminis often delay marrying until quite late in life and frequently choose a mate who is much older than themselves, with less demanding sexual urges.

If you are a woman your ideal man will have money and a position of power, allowing you to mix with the clever, educated people you prefer. Your ideal partner if you are a man is an independently wealthy, older woman, although you won't hesitate to have affairs with younger women, whose attentions boost both your ego and your vanity.
Romance rating: 5

Cancer, the Crab
You may well resemble your sign animal, the crab, in that you hide your soft, vulnerable inner self behind a tough, protective shell. You are in fact very sensitive and easily hurt, and both sexes are prone to tears. Such sensitivity in a man can be very attractive, as it arouses sympathy and brings out the mothering instinct in women, yet it should not be displayed too often or you might be branded a wimp! Cancer women often turn on the tears as a way of breaking down a man's resistance and winning him over.

Your home life is very important to you, and a troubled marriage will make you very unhappy. Few Cancerians care much about the outside world, which they view as a hostile and unpleasant place. If you are unmarried, you may still be living with your parents. And you will be more interested in finding a potential marriage partner than in partying and having a wild time. It's not that you don't enjoy socialising. You do, but you would rather do it as half of a couple, especially in the role of host or hostess.

If you are a woman, nothing gives you greater pleasure

than running your home and taking care of your man. You likewise make a loving, caring mother, although you won't want to have too many children. And because you may have appealing looks and a warm, sympathetic and friendly manner, you are attractive to men, whose egos you are naturally good at massaging.

But if you are a man finding a suitable partner is rather more difficult, because you are untidy, shy and lacking in drive, and you need a woman who combines being a good homemaker with independent wealth or a good income from her job. The worst fault of both sexes is their tendency to criticize and complain. Nothing is ever entirely satisfactory according to a Cancerian.

However, Cancerians marry for keeps and will cling to their mates through thick and thin. It is no accident that they have the lowest divorce rate of all the zodiac types. Romance rating: 4

Leo, the Lion
Like Aries and Sagittarius, Leo is a Fire sign – you are an energetic and outgoing person, who wants to get ahead and make something of your life. Your self-confidence and strong personality enable you to push yourself forward and take command, as there is nothing you like better than running the show. You love being in the spotlight, too – and the sound of applause is music to your ears.

You are probably quite tall, with a lithe physique and an active, yet graceful, way of moving. You may also have large, attractive eyes, and a curly mane of hair. Your lips may, however, be rather thin, and you have a picky, cat-like way of eating. You are naturally sociable, generous and kind, qualities that can bring you a lot of friends and admirers, though you will always want to be at the centre of your social scene.

Your love life is important to you, not only because you tend to fall in love easily, but because having someone respond in kind reinforces your sense of self-importance.

Your romantic involvements quickly become hot and passionate, but like all blazes they soon burn themselves out. You have striking looks and a confident manner, which make your quarry feel lucky to be approached by you. However, your lover will be required to look up to you admiringly, and be totally faithful, as you are a jealous type. Your ego will not allow your lover to even look at another person, let alone sleep with him or her.

Both Leo men and women like being married, but for different reasons. The man regards his home as his lair, with his wife providing the comfort he needs after a hard day pursuing his ambitions. The Leo-born wife may also work – indeed, she usually regards housework as demeaning and boring – yet her home is where she can display both her husband (who will ideally be distinguished in some way) and her talents as a hostess, not to mention her wealth and good taste.

Because the Leo woman will not take second place to any man, she requires a partner in the true sense of the word.

Romance rating: 8

Virgo, the Virgin
You have much in common with Geminians, especially physical appearance. You are typically quite slim, even delicate, in build; your shoulders are broader than those of the average Gemini, though many Virgo men have a rather effeminate physique. Your best facial features are your long, beautifully shaped eyebrows and your high forehead (matching your intelligent mind). You also have sad, gentle, light-coloured eyes, which are particularly appealing to the opposite sex. You are probably not above average height.

You are one of the most careful and cautious of the zodiac types. Allied with your weak sex urge, these characteristics can make you an uncertain, even inhibited, lover. As you are an intellectual, rather than a physical, type, you have to feel a mental attraction to any would-be lover. Because you are a perfectionist, and always need to be in control, you are rarely swept away by love – and you may further hamper your love life by criticizing your partner's less fastidious habits. In fact you are a match for the typical Cancerian when it comes to criticizing and complaining. You are also obsessed with details and can be more than a little self-righteous.

The other side of the coin is that your strong sense of duty and high moral standards usually make you a loyal and attentive partner. Yet, like the Geminian, you are quite capable of hypocrisy. It's not unknown for Virgos to condemn promiscuity in others while indulging in the odd affair themselves. And, being rather calculating, you will only marry someone who has money and who can adequately support you.

Apart from lacking confidence, your frequent anxiety makes it difficult for you to relax with the opposite sex and may prevent you from being a wholly satisfying lover. You are also too ready to blame others for what are really faults in yourself.

You are overly concerned with your health and fitness, and are likely to be a food-faddist and a keep-fit fanatic, neither of which add to your attractiveness. Try to let go more and loosen up!

Romance rating: 2

Libra, the Scales
Librans are typically physically attractive, with regular features and well-formed, sexy bodies, and they add to their natural charms by dressing in smart, stylish clothes and by making sure they are always clean and fresh.

As a Libran, you probably have large, bright, attractive eyes and full, sensuous lips. However, you may also possess thick ankles, and if you are male you may have one or more feminine features, such as narrow shoulders or scant body hair. You dislike getting your hands dirty. Instead you are drawn to occupations – like hairdressing, clothes designing, and selling beauty products – which improve the appearance of others.

You have a pleasant, open, friendly manner, and this, coupled with your love of company and your interest in people, can bring you a wide circle of friends. Your natural politeness and sympathy help you avoid arguments and unpleasantness. Indeed, you go out of your way to be nice. And, though this is usually a good thing, it could prevent you from standing up for yourself when necessary. In fact your dislike of 'causing a scene' may even stop you ending a love affair that has gone sour. If you're not careful, you could end up saddling yourself with a marriage partner who is not right for you.

Despite your popularity with the opposite sex, you tend to keep your emotions under control and you are seldom a passionate or flamboyant lover. If male, women are likely to be charmed by you, and you will enjoy playing the field. Yet while you are initially considerate and thoughtful, you tend to become increasingly undemonstrative as time goes by. If female, men will be as putty in your hands, though none of them will like your indecision if they pop the question.

You are normally a cautious spender where others are concerned, but you don't stint yourself when it comes to clothes, make-up and perfume for personal use, or furniture for your home. However, you will buy expensive presents and throw lavish parties if you need to impress someone who is important to you for business or romance.

Romance rating: 7

Scorpio, the Scorpion

Those born under Scorpio have much in common with Cancerians. Both their sign animals have hard shells, but scorpions also have a sting in their tails. This makes you dangerous to deal with, as any opponent is likely to come off worst.

You probably have a lithe, wiry physique, and you are

not likely to stand above medium height. Your face is broad and strong, with prominent cheekbones, and your nose has a fleshy tip and large nostrils. Your direct, penetrating gaze gives others the impression that you can see into their souls. You walk in an easy, relaxed manner when you are at peace with yourself and the world, but if not you stride about like a stormtrooper! In common with Aries women, the Scorpio female typically has small breasts and more body hair than she would like.

You are an intuitive, emotionally vulnerable type, although you hide these apparent weaknesses behind a tough exterior. Possessing great energy and drive, you will work steadfastly for years to attain your goals – or to take revenge on someone who has done you wrong. And because you love wielding power, you tend to assert yourself as the dominant partner in any relationship.

If female, you have a subtly powerful yet intense sexuality, which makes you attractive to men. Your intuition helps you handle your lovers and also warns you if they cheat on you. Yet your love life is hampered by your temperamental nature, which makes you blow hot and cold, and your preoccupation with your own needs and feelings.

You have a strong sexual urge, though this is normally kept under control. And your main concern is to satisfy your own desires, not those of your partner.

If male, you have a rather cavalier attitude to contraception. Yet if your sexual partner becomes pregnant you are likely to abandon her and claim that the pregnancy is her own fault.

Romance rating: 6

Sagittarius, the Centaur
Like the other two Fire signs, Aries and Leo, you have an outgoing, upbeat personality, although your sense of fun and your love of the good life give you the edge on them, making you the greatest romantic of the zodiac, if not the

best lover in a physical sense (a position held by those born under Capricorn).

If male, you are likely to be quite tall, while the Sagittarius woman is normally of medium height. You have a trim, attractive body when young, but get plump in later life, due to your love of food. Your face is long, with a high, narrow forehead and a prominent nose. Your nostrils tend to flare in moments of excitement and your teeth are large and prominent. These features give you a horsey look, accentuated by the way you toss your head and by your whinnying laugh. You have strong legs with lovely thighs, which you will show off whenever possible. You prefer to wear loose-fitting sporty or casual clothes because you are an outdoor type who likes to feel free and unrestricted.

You generally enjoy company, as you are sociable by nature. You are also good-humoured and generous; in fact you may be something of a spendthrift. You certainly have trouble saving, and you have a weakness for gambling.

Being a bit of a flirt, you particularly enjoy the company of the opposite sex. But you tend to lose your heart too quickly, before finding out whether the new man or woman in your life is really the one for you. However, you are a charming, easy-going, extroverted and fun-loving romantic partner who likes to travel and will happily visit exotic places with your lover.

While you make a wonderful boyfriend or girlfriend, you are not very keen on being tied down in the long term. This is why many married Sagittarians have affairs and why they typically marry more than once.

Despite being the life and soul of the party, you are by no means superficial. You are also interested in the deeper questions of life, and may make a career in law, religion or politics.

Romance rating: 9

Capricorn, the Goat
You are unusual in that you may belong to one of two physical types. The first is taller than average, with more rounded and sensual features, while the second is shorter, with a long face and rather gnomish looks. Both types are quite slim, and have large hands, knees and feet. Capricorn women usually have well-shaped average-size breasts, and the men often have beards.

You are cautious, careful and methodical. You like to know where you are going and dislike having to change your plans. Indeed, you are a quiet, introverted type, who prefers to work alone at your own pace, particularly outdoors.

Some people find you too slow and careful for their taste. And you may try to compensate for your lack of self-confidence by gaining a position of authority. Other people's respect is important to you, even though you like to keep your distance from colleagues, as you are not naturally warm and communicative.

You are perhaps the least romantic of the zodiac types, as you have a rather intellectual approach to the opposite sex. If male, you are unlikely to feel entirely at ease with women, whose emotional needs you find unsettling, although you are prepared to put up with their company if it will help advance your career. Yet as a lover you win hands down over the other signs, as your sign animal – the goat – suggests. Indeed, your strong sex urge can have you playing the field, particularly as a way of avoiding commitment to any one woman. If female, you enjoy being taken out and cosseted, as this makes you feel special. Like your male counterpart you have trouble giving your heart, but when you fall in love you fall deeply, so you need to be sure you've chosen the right man.

Your love life may be disrupted by your strong attachment to your family, and also by the fact that you say what you think. Both sexes are careful with their money (some might say mean). The Capricorn man is unlikely to wine and dine his lover, even though he probably has plenty of cash stashed away.

You feel most relaxed with people older than yourself, whose wisdom and conservatism matches your own. Young people are too lively and unpredictable, and you often feel shy and rather awkward in their company.

Like Scorpios, you never forget a wrong and will wait years if necessary to get your revenge.

Romance rating: 1

Aquarius, the Water-Pourer
You possess the most independent and unconventional character of the twelve zodiac types. You are very changeable, and if someone attempted to pin you down you would probably change again just to keep them guessing.

You probably have quite a tall, lean body, with the same large hands and feet as Capricorns (although yours are better shaped), and broad shoulders. If male, your hair may be thinning, thus emphasizing your dome-shaped head. Female Aquarians, again like their Capricorn cousins, have medium-sized, or smaller, breasts. Both sexes have very unusual dress sense, and if female, you may not bother much with make-up or elaborate hairstyles. You prefer to feel free and unrestricted, and ready to go!

As with the other two Air signs, Gemini and Libra, you are a good conversationalist who enjoys intellectual pursuits. And like them you prefer casual encounters, rather than long-term relationships. You hate the idea of being tied down, so you're likely to put off getting married as long as possible. If male, your girlfriends will find you different and interesting, yet frustrating if they want a commitment. And if female, your boyfriends will probably soon discover that you are cleverer than they are and that you have a number of traditionally masculine interests. Hence you are not a great romantic, although here – as in most other ways – you can surprise.

You prefer to go out with two or more people at the same time. It is very difficult for you to lose your heart completely, and indeed you wouldn't want to, as you realise the emotional risks of falling in love.

When things are going well you can be a lot of fun. You like to laugh, and you can always find interesting things to do. But, against this, you tend to drift off into moody silences, which can be very upsetting for your friends and lovers.

Your strong sex drive means that you sometimes seek sex rather than love, and you tend to spread yourself around instead of sticking to one person. But you are discreet about your affairs and try to avoid hurting any of your lovers.

Romance rating: 4

Pisces, the Fish

You may have a somewhat unprepossessing appearance, being short and plump, with a large, round face. You might also suffer from acne, or bear the scars of an earlier acne outbreak. You have trouble with your clothes, which either don't fit properly or are crumpled and stained, or both. And not only do you suffer from foot problems, but your shoes have a distressing tendency to become scuffed and down-at-heel.

To offset these physical shortcomings, you are blessed with a pleasant, good-natured personality, a fine sense of humour and a generous disposition. In fact you tend to be *too* generous and thus have difficulty in making ends meet. You are also very intuitive and sympathetic, qualities which make you easy to get on with. Less positively, you are a born worrier.

Because you always try to please others, you are an attentive, moderately romantic lover, always prepared to spend money on a date. Even so, your love life is hindered by your shyness and by your lack of self-confidence, which keeps you dithering when you should be making your move. You also have difficulty in making up your mind, and this makes you hesitant about marriage.

Being rather weak and uncertain, you are easily influenced and led astray. As a lover, you are warm, caring and affectionate, and do your best to please and entertain. In fact you hate arguments and disagreements, and will do everything in your power to avoid them.

While you are capable of carrying on more than one love affair at a time, you are unlikely to enjoy the attendant anxiety. And because you are somewhat careless, your deception will eventually be discovered, and you will have to pay the price.

Romance rating: 5

Born on the Cusp?

If your birthday is on one of the first three days or last three days of your sun sign period, you were born on the cusp. This means you have the characteristics of two sun signs, your own and the preceding or succeeding one, depending on whether your birthday falls at the beginning or end of your sun sign period. For instance, if you were born on 21, 22 or 23 March you have mixed Pisces/Aries characteristics, whereas if you were born on 18, 19 or 20 April you have mixed Aries/Taurus characteristics. If you are a cuspal type you should therefore read both your character outlines.

RISING SIGNS

A fuller understanding of your romantic nature can be gained by finding out which sign was rising or ascending above the Eastern horizon at the moment of your birth. Like the sun sign, the ascending sign symbolizes certain aspects of your character.

You can determine your rising sign by following the method below, provided that you know your time of birth (even if it's only approximate). But first you need to convert your birth time to Greenwich Mean Time (GMT).

In Britain, we follow GMT during the autumn and winter, from 2 a.m. on the fourth Sunday in October until

2 a.m. on the third Sunday in March. On that day in March the clocks are put forward by one hour to Summer Time, which continues until the following fourth Sunday in October, when the clocks are put back one hour to GMT. So if you were born during the Summer Time period you must take one hour away from your birth time to convert it to Greenwich Mean Time.

Unfortunately, we have only been changing to Summer Time on the third Sunday in March, and returning to GMT on the fourth Sunday in October, since 1975. Before that year the changeover dates were more variable, with Summer Time sometimes not beginning until 22 April and the return to GMT occasionally taking place as early as 16 September (as it did in 1923).

Those readers who would like to know the exact dates on which the time changes took place should consult my book *Fortune-Telling by Astrology*, which gives them as far back as 1916.

When you have determined your GMT birth time, draw the following figure on a sheet of paper with the added clock times:

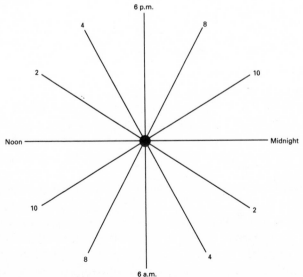

Figure 1

Next, write your sun sign in the segment covering 6 a.m. to 8 a.m., and continue by writing the other zodiac signs, in a clockwise direction, in each segment of the figure. The zodiac sign that falls in the two-hour time segment of your birth is your ascending sign.

For example, someone born on 15 July at 10.30 p.m. must first take one hour away from his birth time. He was therefore born at 9.30 p.m. GMT. As his sun sign is Cancer, he must write 'Cancer' in the 6 a.m. to 8 a.m. segment. Then, by writing in the following zodiac signs in clockwise order around the wheel, he can see that the sign lying in the time period 8 p.m. to 10 p.m. is Aquarius. He is therefore a Cancer native with an Aquarius ascendant.

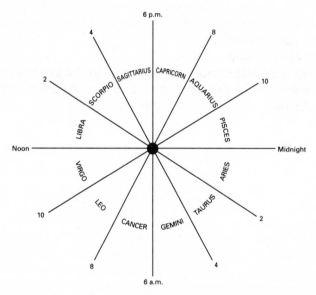

Figure 2 A Cancerian born at 9.30am GMT has an Aquarian ascendant.

When you have determined your own ascending sign, you should read the character outline for that sign. You will probably recognize quite a few of your own characteristics. Indeed, many astrologers regard the ascending sign as more important than the sun sign in determining (or symbolizing) one's character and appearance.

If you were born at or around sunrise, your sun sign and rising sign are the same. You are therefore a double Aries, a double Gemini, or whatever, and you will have the characteristics associated with that sign developed to the full, unless some other influence was introduced by being born on a cusp.

FINDING YOUR IDEAL PARTNER

Your ascendant is also important because it tells you what type of person you are most attracted to, and it could give you an insight into who would be your most compatible marriage partner.

To find this out, all you need to do is note which sign is exactly opposite your ascending sign in the wheel you have drawn. In Figure 2, for example, the sign opposite Aquarius is Leo, which means that the person concerned will be drawn to those with a Leo sun sign or, more probably, rising sign.

A less precise guide to someone's attractiveness and compatibility can be gained from your sun sign. As we have seen, the twelve signs are arranged in four groups – 'fiery', 'airy', 'earthy' or 'watery'. As a general rule, the Fire signs (Aries, Leo and Sagittarius) are most compatible with Air signs (Gemini, Libra and Aquarius), and vice versa, in the same way that fire needs air to burn, while air is heated and moved by fire. Similarly, the Earth signs (Taurus, Virgo and Capricorn) are most compatible with the Water signs (Cancer, Scorpio and Pisces), and vice versa, in the same way that water moistens and so makes the earth fertile, while earth gives water a home.

Of the three in question, the sun sign best suited to you is the one lying opposite your sun sign in Figure 2. Or you can look at the chart on page 22.

FIRE SIGNS	AIR SIGNS
Aries⟷Libra	
Leo⟷Aquarius	
Sagittarius⟷Gemini	

EARTH SIGNS	WATER SIGNS
Taurus⟷Scorpio	
Virgo⟷Pisces	
Capricorn⟷Cancer	

To get a really accurate idea of romantic compatability both partners need to have their birth charts drawn up and compared by an experienced astrologer. This is quite common in the East but relatively unknown in the West. Unlike arranged marriages, Western couples get married because they love each other. But love, as we have seen, often behaves like a mischievous child. When the first flush of romance fades away the loved one may start to show their true colours and that marriage made in heaven may end in tears. Why not try to avoid some of the heartache by finding out as much as you can about your partner's character *before* you take the plunge?

Chapter 2

PASSION IN THE PALMS

When a man and a woman hold hands in public, it is one of the best signs that they are emotionally close, perhaps even in love. Interestingly, most married couples prefer to walk separately, or the woman might take hold of the man's arm, as if for support.

Couples who have just started going out together also walk apart, yet join hands occasionally, if they have to cross a busy street or face some other hazard together. Indeed, hand-holding is the first step along the road to deeper intimacy, bringing two naked skin surfaces together, while demonstrating the couple's togetherness. Couples who are lovers, by contrast, often walk with an arm around each other's waist, which brings greater physical contact.

The act of hand-holding has a deeper meaning, however, because the hands – by their shape, colour, fleshiness and pattern of lines – are living symbols of ourselves, representing our character, temperament, health and life pattern or fate. Your life is truly in your own hands! When you take hold of someone else's hand, you are in a sense pressing your life against theirs. And who knows where a bit of hand-holding may end? Perhaps even in marriage?

This chapter tells you how you can interpret your own hands to find out more about your emotional type and your emotional needs, as well as likely long-term relationships or marriages, numbers of children and so on. If you then apply what you learn to the hands of someone you like or love, you will not only be able to understand their character better but will be in a better position to judge if they are the right partner for you. You will certainly gain a far deeper insight into them than you would from going out together on a few dates.

The main areas and lines of the hands are shown in Figure 3. The fleshy mounts together form the palms. The largest and most important from a romantic point of view is the mount of Venus below the thumb, and the mount of the moon just next to it. The thumb and the fingers share the name of the mount at their base, which derive from mythology, the thumb being the digit of Venus; the first or index finger, of Jupiter; the second finger, of Saturn;

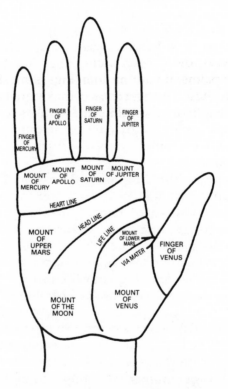

Figure 3 The principal areas and lines of the hand.

the third finger, of the sun or Apollo; and the fourth or little finger, of Mercury. This naming system also links the fingers with the planets that share their names, which are said to rule them.

HAND SHAPES

You can get an immediate insight into your basic character by identifying your overall hand shape. The ancient system of palmistry recognizes four primary hand shapes, each of which is linked with one of the four elements, Fire, Air, Earth and Water.

To determine your hand type, you need to consider the shape of your palms and the length of your fingers. First, look at your palms to see if they are square or rectangular in shape. Next, compare the length of your fingers with that of your palms. If your middle fingers are shorter than your palms, they are short, but if they equal or perhaps exceed the length of your palms, they are long.

You should now be able to identify your hand type from the following list:
1) rectangular palms with short fingers = Fire hands
2) square palms with long fingers = Air hands
3) square palms with short fingers = Earth hands
4) rectangular palms with long fingers = Water hands.
The character traits associated with these four hand types are outlined below.

1) Fire Hands (Rectangular palms, short fingers)
You are essentially an outgoing, lively person who likes change and variety. You are always ready to accept a new challenge, though you need to work in your own way and, ideally, to be the leader. In fact, you resent authority and freedom is very important to you.

But your tendency to rush in can involve you with unsavoury people and impractical schemes. While you are naturally enthusiastic, you are also excitable and impatient, sometimes even bad-tempered and aggressive.

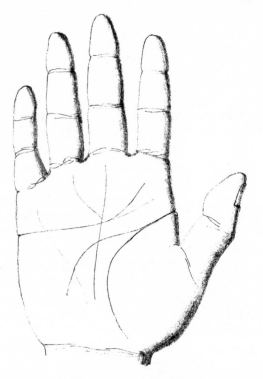

Figure 4 The Fire hand.

When things are going well you are cheerful and expansive – and like to laugh. You enjoy dressing in eye-catching, colourful clothes which help you stand out in a crowd. And your innate self-confidence means that you are more of a chaser in love than a sit-back-and-wait person. Your sociability and sense of fun help you attract friends and lovers, but you are not particularly faithful (preferring variety to constancy). You may be vocal and quite creative, though what you say is seldom backed by much deep thought.

2) *Air Hands (Square palms, long fingers)*

You have the same love of freedom and independence as the Fire hand type but you are far more careful and thoughtful in your attitudes. In other words, you prefer to look long and hard before you leap. Whereas the Fire hand type needs freedom of action, you require freedom of thought and expression. You are basically an intellectual, deep-thinking type who loves solving problems and can tackle nitty-gritty details.

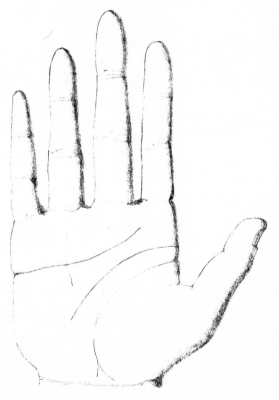

Figure 5 The Air hand.

You also like to talk and expound your views rather than get physically or emotionally involved with others.

In fact real intimacy disturbs you. While you give the
impression of being bright, cheerful and optimistic, you
lack true inner warmth. And because you find disorder of
any sort distressing, you are inclined to be finicky, precise
and over-conscientious. You have artistic talents, notably
verbal or expressive (perhaps as an actor, writer or public
speaker), and you are drawn to politics and psychiatry.
Because you lack the outgoing self-confidence of the Fire
hand person, you are less well-equipped to take the lead
in love, though love and sex don't really interest you all
that much.

3) Earth Hands (Square palms, short fingers)
This hand type is usually fleshier and less flexible than
Fire and Air hands, and betokens a steadier, more practi-

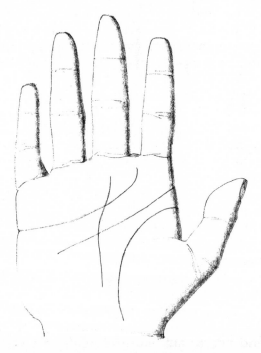

Figure 6 The Earth hand.

cal and down-to-earth nature. You are a calm, reliable person rather than an adventurer who seeks new challenges, and some might find you a little dull and predictable. You enjoy working with your hands, particularly with natural materials like wood and stone, and if you have a creative bent, you may be drawn to sculpture, pottery or wood-carving.

Order and control are important to you. Indeed, you are upset by sudden change, and do your best to avoid it. You may be a bit of a plodder but you are also honest and dependable. And because you are home-loving, you make a good marriage partner for another Earth hand type or those with Water hands. You normally get on well with others, as you are loving and warm-hearted, and your explosive bad temper only comes out when you are pushed over the edge. You have a strong sex drive and a need for both physical and emotional closeness, yet your lack of self-confidence can stop you being the initiator in love. As one might expect, you are at your best in a settled relationship, where all is comfortable and familiar.

4) Water Hands (Rectangular palms, long fingers)
You have the same need for order and calm as the Earth hand person. Yet, lacking his practicality and drive, you may have trouble achieving what you want. You are in fact something of a dreamer, dwelling more in your imagination than in the real world, yet at the same time being sensitive to what goes on around you. Indeed, your heightened sensitivity makes you very aware of other people's feelings and moods, which helps you understand and sympathize with them, although you may not be able to give them much practical advice.

Because you are a follower, not a leader, you find it difficult to push yourself forward in love, preferring to be pursued rather than pursuing. You are temperamentally best suited to partner an Earth hand person. Like you, Earth hand people are not afraid of emotional commitment and their practical skills can help you turn some of

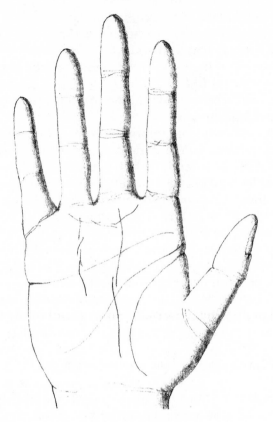

Figure 7 The Water hand.

your dreams into reality. Fire or Air hand people are too changeable and unemotional for you, and they in turn would find your moody – not to say depressive – tendencies difficult to deal with.

A Water hand woman would make an ideal wife for an Earth hand man, but the reverse combination would be less successful because Water hand men lack drive and determination. They are therefore unlikely to get very far in their careers which would trouble an Earth hand woman. All in all, you are a dependent type who needs to be looked after and cosseted if you are to be happy.

The temperaments of these four hand types match those described earlier for the four astrological groups. So a Fire hand person has the same basic temperament as someone born under one of the Fire signs (Aries, Leo and Sagittarius); an Air hand person has the same basic temperament as someone born under one of the Air signs (Gemini, Libra and Aquarius); an Earth hand person has much in common with someone born under one of the Earth signs (Taurus, Virgo and Capricorn); while a Water hand person has similar traits to a person born under one of the Water signs (Cancer, Scorpio and Pisces). In fact it is likely that, if you have, say, Fire hands, you were born under one of the Fire signs.

But what if your hand type does not match your sun-sign group? As I explained in the previous chapter, your character and other attributes are not only symbolized by your sun sign, but also by your ascending sign, whose influence is often predominant. And your rising sign may belong to a different group from your sun sign.

For example, if you have Water hands but were born under a Fire sign, then you will almost certainly have a rising Water sign, whose effects will dilute the fiery characteristics of the sun sign. This will explain why you don't feel like, behave like, or even look like, a typical Aries, Leo or Sagittarius. You will be a Water person, as your hands indicate, yet you will have more drive and determination (which are Fire characteristics) than the typical Water individual.

OTHER HAND FEATURES

Each hand type must be interpreted along with a number of other hand features for a deeper understanding of their owner's personality. For example, are your hands warm, dry and (if you are European) pink in colour? These are all positive indicators, representing emotional warmth, a lack of anxiety and general good health. Or are they cold, damp and white? Cold hands are almost always white in colour, and both features reveal a colder, and therefore less emotional, personality.

If a Fire hand type has cold, white hands, he or she is less open, generous and emotionally warm than the hand type by itself would suggest. Such a person would certainly be more ruthless than someone with warm, pink Fire hands, and in matters of love is more likely to be a heartless seducer or manipulative mistress than a caring lover.

Cold, white Air hands belong to a very emotionally repressed person, the type who can plan all manner of grandiose schemes without taking into account their effect on other people.

Cold, white Earth hand types have a stronger and more insistent sex drive than those with either Air or Water hands, yet their lack of emotional warmth tends to drive them into loveless sexual encounters. A man of this type would probably be unfaithful.

Those with cold, white Water hands tend to have a passive, introverted personality and a low self-esteem. They may believe that they aren't very lovable.

Moist hands typically belong to the person who is chronically anxious and has a poor self-image. Dry hands, by contrast, suggest a far more positive and confident personality. Moist hands are unpleasant to touch, and usually, although by no means only, belong to those with Water hands.

Occasionally they are also possessed by the least confident Fire hand types but it is rare for either Air or Earth hand types to have moist hands because Air hand people are relatively unemotional, while Earth hand people have stable emotions. Hence if either of these types have moist palms they are particularly troubled and need to be handled with care, as one can never tell how they are going to react or behave.

FINGERS AND FINGER NAILS

The length, smoothness or knottiness, thickness, and setting of the fingers must also be considered, as these features can modify the characteristics suggested by the hand type.

Short fingers always signify quick reactions and impatience with detail, whereas long fingers indicate a more considered approach to life and an ability, even a need, to take care of details. Hence short-fingered people are more open and spontaneous, and are less likely to be critical, than those with long fingers. The shorter the fingers compared to the palm length, the more pronounced are these traits, with very short fingers suggesting an unreliable, irresponsible character. Similarly, very long fingers mark out the person who is indecisive, sluggish in thought and a nit-picker.

As a companion, the short-fingered person is easier to get along with and more fun than the long-fingered person, who will watch what he or she spends, prefer intellectual pleasures to those of the senses, and be unwilling to try anything new or adventurous. These traits are worse in the person whose fingers are both long and thin. Thick fingers reveal a more sensual dimension to the personality, though it will still lack the short-fingered person's spontaneity. And because he or she is more suspicious than the short-fingered type, he is more likely to accuse you of infidelity.

When the knuckles are barely visible, so that the fingers have a general smoothness of line, the person is more quick-thinking, intuitive, impulsive, and sensitive to their surroundings. Those with short, smooth fingers are therefore very open, outgoing, friendly and fun-loving types. Yet, because they tend to be poor organizers, they are also often untidy and unreliable. They are prone to lose things like addresses and telephone numbers, yet they will always breeze in with a plausible excuse for their lateness or disorganization.

Those with long fingers that are also smooth have greater mental agility than is suggested by the finger length alone. Hence they are more fluent in their speech and open in their behaviour, and are less likely to be carping and critical. However, long fingers are typically knotted rather than smooth, which indicates opposite tendencies. In fact long, knotted fingers belong to people of reason and analysis, who are careful in all that they do, correct in their manner, tidy and punctual.

While not that much fun, they are far more dependable than those with short, smooth fingers, but they cannot lose their hearts as readily, nor are they capable of behaving romantically. If your partner has long, knotted fingers don't expect them to turn up out of the blue, clutching a bottle of champagne, ready to whisk you off on a midnight cruise. Gestures like this are beyond them. But while they cannot offer the excitement of grand passion they can certainly give you the security of long-term affection.

Your prospective partner's fingernails can also give you all sorts of clues to their personality. The ideal nails are smooth, healthily pink in colour, glistening, have visible moons and no white flecks. These features taken together indicate good health, a stable temperament, and an optimistic, outgoing disposition. Their nails should also be clean and unbroken. Dirty and unmanicured fingernails reveal a poor self-image and sloppy, untidy habits. Their owner is unlikely to make a suitable partner. The same can be said of the person whose nails have one or more of the following defects: dullness, white flecks, no moons or very large ones, perpendicular ridges, and are thin, or pale in colour. All these features signify character and health problems that could cause difficulties in a relationship.

Beware also of the person who has fingernails that are shorter than their width (meaning that part of the nail that is attached to the finger itself). Such a person has an irritable, argumentative, critical nature, and if such nails grow on short fingers he or she could be rash, headstrong, impulsive, prone to outbursts of temper when frustrated, and even violent.

Fingernails that are longer than their width, by contrast, symbolize a far more easy-going and even-tempered disposition. When the fingernails are triangular or fan-shaped they signify anxiety and nervousness. Those with such nails rarely feel at ease, and tend to be overly concerned with their health, financial security, and what the neighbours think.

The most fortunate fingers are either set on a level or on a gentle slope at the top of the palm. They are straight, and the index finger and third finger are equal in length, or the index finger extends to the base of the middle finger's nail. Fingers like this reveal a good self-image, a realistic and balanced view of one's talents, and a lack of deviousness. Those whose fingers depart from this ideal may have psychological difficulties and a sense of inadequacy.

The fingers that are most important in evaluating a potential partner are the first or index fingers (known to palmists as the Jupiter fingers) and the fourth or little fingers (traditionally called the Mercury fingers). The index fingers reveal how a person views and judges himself, and the fourth fingers symbolize his or her sexual nature.

When the ends of the Jupiter fingers reach to the base of the fingernails of the middle (or Saturn) fingers, it shows that the person has a realistic view of himself. He does not have either a big head or an inferiority complex.

If, however, the index fingers are short, so that their ends do not reach the base of the middle fingers' nails, then the person has a greater or lesser sense of inferiority according to the shortness of the fingers. Those with an inferiority complex feel inadequate, which makes them susceptible to feelings of jealousy, suspicion and envy. They also find it impossible to laugh at themselves or to admit that they are wrong. It is no coincidence that some of the worst tyrants in history have had short index fingers. Saddam Hussein is a prime example of a tyrant

whose sense of personal inadequacy has spurred him on
to attain supreme power.

Conversely, the person with an inferiority complex may
be so lacking in confidence that he fails to make any effort,
believing that he is not good enough or talented enough
to advance in life. His frustration can lead to anger and
violence in personal relationships.

When the ends of the index fingers reach above the
base of the middle fingers' nails it indicates that the
person believes himself to be cleverer or more talented
than he actually is. In fact he is the archetypal big head,
which causes problems in his personal relationships and
in his work. He (or she) will probably think he is doing
you a favour by going out with you, and his behaviour
towards you, as with his colleagues at work, is likely to be
arrogant and imperious. Nothing will ever be his fault,
whereas you – poor, untalented, dim-witted you – will
always be to blame. Such a person, whether male or
female, is best avoided, unless you also have long Jupiter
fingers and can match him (or her) in arrogance.

The index fingers should also be straight, indicating a
proper balance between the ego and the conscience,
symbolized by the middle or Saturn fingers. Yet quite
often the index fingers bend towards or away from the
middle fingers, revealing an abnormal relationship
between ego and conscience.

Should the index fingers bend inwards, the person has
a strong conscience, which closely controls his ego. A little
self-control is not such a bad thing, but if his conscience
has been formed by strict, old-fashioned parents, who
disapprove of sex, he may not be able to relax in his
lovemaking or be able to follow anything other than a
conventional path through life. Furthermore, if his conscience tells him he must 'get ahead', he will single-
mindedly pursue success, but he may also become a
workaholic, who is unable to enjoy life (see Figure 8).

As might be expected, when the index fingers bend
away from the middle fingers, they symbolize the person

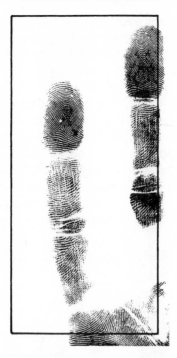

Figure 8 Index finger bending towards middle finger.

whose ego is unrestrained by his conscience. He is a free agent, so to speak. Hence he does what he likes, when he likes, and shows little concern for how his actions might affect others. At worst, he might get involved in criminal activities, although it is perhaps more likely that he will tell lies, be unfaithful, take your money, and generally make use of you. He gets away with all this selfishness because his great charm stops people from seeing him as he really is. These tendencies will be worse in the person whose index fingers are both too long and which bend outwards, for here we have arrogance combined with unscrupulousness, which is a dangerous mixture.

The little fingers (also known as the fourth or Mercury fingers) are very important in evaluating our attitude to sex and how we conduct our sexual relationships. You should look at your own, in order to understand yourself better in these respects, and also at those of your potential partner. But do bear in mind that the little fingers are not the only indicators of these aspects; they should be interpreted alongside the mounts of Venus and the heart lines, which also relate to sexual attitudes.

The little fingers, like the other fingers, should ideally be straight, and should extend, when viewed from the front, to the first knuckle line of the third fingers (see Figure 9). They should be neither too thick nor too thin, and they should have a smooth outline. When they have these positive features they reveal both a normal sex drive and an ability to form satisfactory sexual relationships.

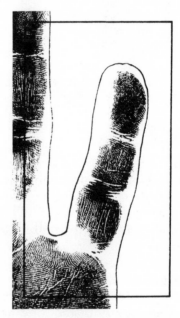

Figure 9 Straight little finger of normal length.

When the little fingers have a less ideal form – by being too long or too short, for example, or by showing an abnormal bend or twist, or by having a low setting – then there is usually some problem with sexual abilities and/or attitudes which will prevent the person being a fully satisfying sexual partner.

Your emotions are symbolized by your third fingers. If these are straight and extend to the base of the nails of your middle fingers, they show that you have balanced and stable emotions. Hence if your little fingers stand close to your third fingers your sexual desires and emotional responses are closely linked, and it is difficult, if not impossible, for you to have sex without being emotionally involved.

However, if someone's hands show a noticeable space between the little fingers and the third fingers (see Figure 10), their sexual desires are kept separate from their emotions, and they will find it difficult to become emotionally involved with their sexual partner. Indeed, such a person will probably have many sexual partners, as sex for him or her is simply a physical act.

It also means that, if you become intimately involved

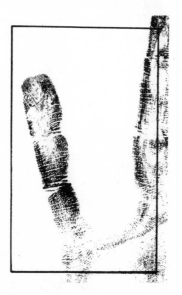

Figure 10 Wide space between little finger and third finger.

with someone like this, he (or she) won't become bonded to you by such intimacy. This will make it comparatively easy for him to be unfaithful or to leave you for another. The wider the space between the little fingers and the third fingers, the greater the inability to become emotionally involved. Hence it is not surprising to find that the hands of many womanizers show such isolated little fingers.

Short little fingers, like short fingers in general, indicate an impatience with detail and a tendency to rush into things. So this person will probably want to start a sexual relationship quickly, and may be a hurried and possibly dissatisfying lover. Long little fingers, by contrast, reveal opposite tendencies and hence belong to the person who is shyer and more diffident. He will be slower and more careful in bed but he will need encouragement if you are to get the best out of him!

When the little fingers are thick they show a strong sexual urge, while if they are thin or waisted they indicate a weaker sex drive and a more hesitant nature. Short, thick little fingers therefore belong to the person who is likely to need sex often and won't care much who he (or she) has it with.

You should also take careful note of the setting of the little fingers. Ideally their bases should be on the same level as those of the third fingers. Sometimes, however, the little fingers are set down so that they arise noticeably lower on the hand than the third fingers (see Figure 11). This low setting symbolizes a parent fixation, which is greater the lower the little fingers are placed.

An individual with a parent fixation will unconsciously seek a partner who most resembles his mother (if a man), or her father (if a woman), in manner and attitudes, and sometimes in looks. The person will want a similar relationship in marriage to that which they had with the parent as a child, which means that he (or she) will expect to be looked after and cared for both physically and emotionally.

Figure 11 Low-set, inward-bending little finger.

This is partly why young women sometimes marry men old enough to be their fathers, especially if the men are rich and can offer them the same security that daddy did when they were children. Inevitably there are problems. Their partner may not live up to their memories of daddy, or they may fail to find a suitable daddy replica and so lead increasingly lonely and emotionally unsatisfying lives. Men seeking substitute mothers have a slightly better time of it, as it is easier for a woman to slip into the mothering role.

The little fingers also symbolize the ability to communicate, especially verbally. When they are short they signify an impulsive, outspoken manner. Combined with their customary impatience, such qualities may mean that the person has difficulty in talking things over calmly and rationally. They may have problems with expression in general, and hence poor communication skills. Long little fingers, contrarily, symbolize verbal fluency and a love of talking, but often an associated inability to make decisions or take action. Little fingers that reach to the first knuckle line of the third fingers signify both a facility with words and the ability to make decisions and take action, if necessary.

You are probably a charming and persuasive talker if the first, or fingernail, section of your little fingers is the longest of the three. If the fingers are also slightly longer than normal, and if they bend towards the third fingers, then you possess great tact and a natural diplomatic sense (see Figure 12). Others can tell you intimate secrets without fear of being betrayed. But should your little fingers lean away from the third fingers, you are likely to be a blabbermouth who cannot be trusted.

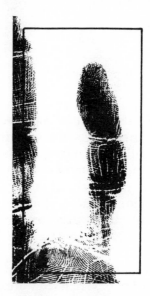

Figure 12 Inward-bending little finger with long nail phalanx.

Little fingers that are twisted signify dishonesty. Such people are 'economical with the truth' – treat any of their stories or promises with caution.

Finally, beware of people who wear rings on one or both of their little fingers. Any ring worn for purely decorative reasons, as opposed to one worn to satisfy convention (such as an engagement ring or a wedding ring) generally symbolizes the person's unease about those qualities which the finger represents. As our little fingers are connected with our sexual desires, a ring on one or both of them can indicate sexual anxiety.

The larger the ring, the greater the problem. Indeed, their anxiety or guilt often makes it difficult for such people to cope with relationships. A ring worn on the left-hand fourth finger shows an inherited or subconscious disquiet about sex, while one worn on the right-hand little finger reveals an acquired difficulty. Those wearing such rings may of course have many good qualities, but you should be aware of their problems in this particular area.

THE VENUS MOUNTS AND THE LIBIDO

The areas below the thumbs, known as the mounts of Venus, are normally the largest and most prominent of the palm mounts. Their inner border is formed by the life line. Ideally they should extend to the middle of the palm, be well-rounded, pink in colour, and firm without being hard (see Figure 13). These positive features signify a healthy constitution, an outgoing disposition, and an active, but not excessive, libido.

When the Venus mounts are less fully formed, the physical energy and the libido are correspondingly weaker. Flat Venus mounts, for example, indicate lethargy and indolence, resulting from poor digestion and a slow metabolism. And if they are also narrow, white and hard, there is little vitality, the personality is lack-lustre and introverted, and the sex drive weak. Such a person is not only prone to psychological disorders, but also to infectious diseases and other physical complaints (see Figure 14).

Very prominent mounts of Venus, especially if they are dark red, reveal a tendency toward excess, deriving from a

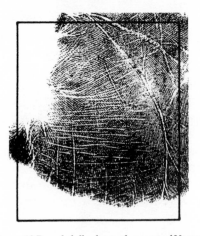

Figure 13 Broad, fully-formed mount of Venus.

hyperactive metabolism. Such people are not only greedy, but also have strong sexual urges, which they will find particularly hard to control if they also have short, thick little fingers. Not only will they spend recklessly, smoke and drink too much, and generally behave in ways that endanger their health, but they are also likely to get themselves into trouble with their sexual antics.

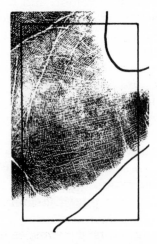

Figure 14 Narrow, deficient mount of Venus.

The upper boundary of the Venus mount is sometimes marked by a line that runs from the edge of the hand above the thumb towards the life line. If present it divides the mount of Venus from the mount of Lower Mars above (see Figure 15). This is called the mother line and, as the name suggests, it reveals a strong maternal influence, which is greater the longer and more deeply marked the line. When this line accompanies low-set little fingers on a man's hand, the mother fixation is emphasized, perhaps to the extent that it will prevent him from ever forming a satisfactory relationship with another woman, and may stop him leaving home.

Figure 15 The Via Mater or Mother line.

THE HEART LINES AND YOUR SEXUALITY

The heart line runs across the palm from the outer edge of the hand towards the mount of Jupiter, which is positioned beneath the index finger (see Figure 16). In their ideal form both heart lines are clearly and quite deeply marked, are long and pink in colour, and are free of breaks and islands. Heart lines like this symbolize a strong and healthy heart and an efficient circulatory system.

Before we examine their characteristics in detail, you need to realize that the left and right hands reveal different aspects of the personality. The left hand displays those traits and physical characteristics that are inherited from our parents, whereas the right hand shows how

Figure 16 Heart line running to mount of Jupiter.

these have been modified by our upbringing and environment to create the people we are now.

This should be kept in mind when considering all hand features. For example a person may have a left-hand index finger of normal length, representing a balanced self-image, but they may also have a short right-hand index finger, indicating an inferiority complex. This shows that, while they were born with the potential to develop a balanced self-image, their ego was somehow stunted in childhood, so that they grew to adulthood feeling inferior. Because the inferiority is acquired, it would probably respond to suitable psychiatric treatment, which would allow them to develop a fairly normal ego balance.

I shall concentrate here on the right-hand heart line because this reveals your social and sexual nature as it appears in your life. To understand your inner social and sexual nature, you must examine your left-hand heart line and note how or whether they differ. The inner and outer you may be mirror images, or you may be a wolf in sheep's clothing!

If your right-hand heart line is of normal length, it will extend across your palm as far, or almost as far, as the mount of Jupiter. And the course it takes will reveal your sexual type.

A heart line with a strong upward curve, which ends on the mount of Saturn or perhaps between the index and middle fingers (see Figure 17), shows that you have a very physical, active sexuality. In other words, you are hot-blooded, easily aroused, and enjoy physical contact. When such a heart line is accompanied by a short, thick little finger and by a plump, firm mount of Venus, the person has a strong and frequent sex urge. Lovemaking is lusty but quick and their satisfaction is derived solely from the physical side of sex.

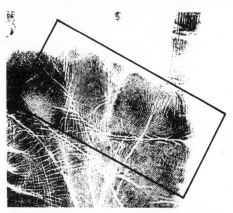

Figure 17 Heart line running to the mount of Saturn.

But if you have a straight heart line (like that shown in Figure 18) which ends either on the base of the Jupiter mount or perhaps curves downwards to meet or even cross the head line, your sexuality is intellectual or passive in nature. Your sexual desires are not excited by sight or touch alone. Your mind has to be involved along with your body. This usually means that you need a bit of romantic interaction with your partner before you are ready for sex. Also, you may sometimes find that you get turned on when doing things that are not in themselves particularly sexy, such as listening to music or walking along a beach. This is probably because they are linked in your mind, possibly subconsciously, with a pleasurable sexual experience you once had.

Figure 18 Straight heart line curving downwards at its end to meet and cross the head line.

If you, as a man, are hoping to seduce a particular woman, or, vice versa, you need to take these two extremes of sexual attitude into account. If the woman in question has an upwardly curving heart line, she will be more receptive to a direct, even physical approach; whereas if her heart line is straight she probably won't like being touched or kissed until you have appealed to her romantically. In other words she will need wooing. While this type of woman is harder to seduce, she is far more likely to be faithful than the first type. But do remember to consider the other indicators of sexuality mentioned earlier.

A heart line that is more gently curved, and which typically ends somewhere on the mount of Jupiter, signifies a sexual attitude that falls somewhere between the two extremes, with both physical and mental elements forming part of the sexual pattern (see Figure 16).

Next, you should examine the two spaces marked A and B in Figure 19, in your own hands.

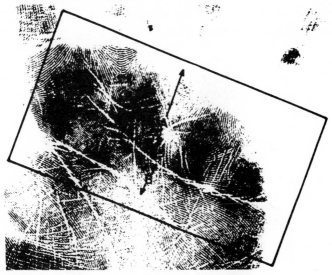

Figure 19 Distances A and B.

If your heart line is low set, so that space A is wide, it shows that you have a warm, outgoing, generous and sympathetic nature. Conversely, when this space is narrow, the character is less open and friendly, and more selfish.

Should the space between your heart line and head line (distance B) be narrow, it implies that you are rather introverted, emotionally cold and selfish. But if wide, it shows that you are extroverted and broadminded, and also altruistic. Hence both space A and space B should ideally be fairly wide.

MARRIAGES AND CHILDREN

The marriage lines are short lines found on the side of the hands between the fourth finger and the start of the heart line (see Figure 20); they normally run on to the mount of Mercury. Each signifies a serious love relationship or marriage, which starts at the time of life indicated by the line's position. The lower a particular line is set, the earlier the relationship or marriage happens; the higher it lies, the later the union occurs.

Figure 20 The marriage lines.

Unfortunately, the age signified by the marriage lines is always difficult to determine precisely. This is because the small distance between the heart line and the little finger represents the whole of your life, which may be short or long or somewhere in between. Using an average lifespan of 75 years, a marriage line appearing at its mid-point will represent a marriage at approximately 37. Marriage lines in different positions need to have their age value calculated in a similar way.

Ideally, you will have only one straight, clearly marked marriage line, free of defects, which will naturally symbolize one happy and long-lasting union. But if two or more are present, it is useful to examine their features to understand why the earlier relationships may have failed or will perhaps fail.

If a marriage line divides to form a fork (see Figure 21), it usually means the marriage breaks down because the couple fall out of love and gradually drift apart. They may of course remain together, but the union will probably be loveless and unhappy. When the fork appears near the start of the marriage line the breakdown may take place quite soon, but if it occurs further along the line the emotional distancing is likely to happen later.

When a bubble-like island appears in a marriage line

Figure 21 Marriage line ending in a fork.

(see Figure 22), it symbolizes a time of difficulty and unhappiness, which will last for a period proportional to the length of the island. Though negative in meaning, a single island does show that the trouble is eventually overcome. This is not the case, however, when a series of small islands form a 'chain' in the marriage line, as this feature usually signifies a long period of unhappiness without resolution.

Figure 22 Marriage line with an island.

Small lines that run downwards from a marriage line are indicators of unhappiness, disappointment and regret, which is worse the more of these lines there are (see Figure 23).

Figure 23 Marriage line with small, downward-running lines.

A marriage line that shows a clear break indicates that the love relationship or marriage may end suddenly and probably finally (see Figure 24). However, if the broken ends of the line overlap one another, then there will probably be a period of separation and its attendant unhappiness, but the couple will eventually sort out their differences and get back together again.

Figure 24 Broken marriage line.

If a marriage line is cut through by a short bar line, this usually symbolizes some outside influence or problem that threatens the stability of the marriage (see Figure 25). Similarly, when a marriage line is terminated by a cross, the marriage will probably be ended by adultery. A star at the end of a marriage line shows that the marriage is likely to come to a sudden and spectacular conclusion.

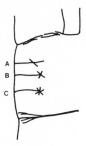

Figure 25 Marriage line A) cut by short bar line; B) ended by a cross: and C) ended by a star.

If a marriage line bends downwards, especially if it ends at the heart line, the marriage may end with the death of the spouse (see Figure 26).

Figure 26 Downward-bending marriage line.

However, when a marriage line is thin at its start but then gradually thickens as the line runs on to the mount of Mercury (see Figure 27), the marriage gets off to a shaky start but things improve and love deepens in time. By contrast, a marriage that begins very well is shown by two short lines at the beginning which meet and merge into one. If the line continues straight on to the mount of Mercury, without defects, the marriage will almost certainly continue to be happy and satisfying. And if the marriage line has small branch lines rising up obliquely from it, these signify the happiness that the marriage or love affair brings.

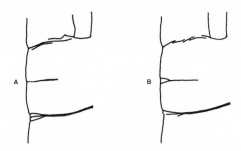

Figure 27 Marriage line A) thickening as it runs on to the mount of Mercury, and B) starting as two short lines that meet and merge into one.

Small branch lines that rise vertically from a marriage line, and which must be distinguished from those that rise up obliquely, each signify a child from that marriage, the thicker and more deeply marked lines representing boys, the thinner ones girls (see Figure 28).

Figure 28 Marriage line with indicators of children.

When a break or an island follows immediately after an uprising line signifying a child, it means that the birth of the baby will cause problems for the couple which will in some way threaten the marriage.

There are two other signs in the hand that symbolize children, the first of which is probably the most reliable.

If you look at the lowest line circling the base of your right thumb, you may notice that it has one or more islands. If so, don't worry, as in this situation the islands are not negative; indeed, each signifies a child, the larger ones boys, the smaller ones girls (see Figure 29). An island placed low down on the line represents a child born when you were (or are) quite young. Higher set islands refer to children born later in life.

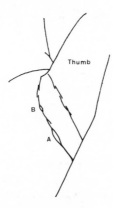

Figure 29 Islands signifying children, A) a boy, B) a girl.

Short vertical, or almost vertical, lines are sometimes present on the base of the mount of Venus. These likewise symbolize children, the longer and thicker ones boys, the shorter, thinner ones girls (see Figure 30).

Figure 30 Lines on mount of Venus indicating children.

Chapter 3
THE LATIN LOVER

There is no head so full of stratagem as that of a libidinous man.

Joseph Addison (1672–1719)

The original Latin Lover was a man named Publius Ovidius Naso, who was born on 20 March, 43 BC, in the little town of Sulmo (now called Sulmona), Italy. He became one of the most gifted poets of his generation and his interest in poetry was rivalled only by his interest in love and sex. Indeed his intuitive understanding of women and his skill in gaining their hearts led him to compose a long poem which advised would-be lovers on how to secure affection and favours from their loved one. The work, entitled *Ars Amatoria* (*The Art of Love*), is the first and possibly most useful ever written on this topic. Its recommendations are as valid now as when it was first published, in the year before Christ's birth.

We know Publius Ovidius Naso better as Ovid. He was of course a Roman, and the language in which he spoke and wrote was Latin. It comes as no surprise to learn that he was born on 20 March. This makes him a cuspal Pisces-Aries, having both the sensitivity of the Pisces-born, which enabled him to write poetry, and the push and strong sex drive of the Aries-born, which produced his second obsession.

Coincidentally, his surname Naso means 'Big Nose', which indicates that one of his ancestors was well-endowed in the nasal area and probably therefore also well-endowed elsewhere, with an active libido. Ovid did not possess his ancestor's large nose but he did inherit his sexual urges. Indeed, he had a total of three wives and a mistress named Corinna, as well as many shorter-lived affairs.

Ovid was not at all bashful about declaring his talent for making women fall in love with him. In fact he regarded himself as an expert. But the advice he gives in his poem shows that he was not simply a one-night-stand merchant. He wanted both to win a woman's heart and keep it, and to sexually satisfy her:

> You, who in Cupid's roll inscribe your name,
> First seek an object worthy of your flame;
> Then strive with art your lady's mind to gain;
> And, last, provide your love may long remain.
> On these three precepts all your work shall move;
> *These are the rules and principles of love.*
> Before your youth with marriage is oppress'd,
> Make choice of one who suits your humour best;
> And such a damsel drops not from the sky:
> She must be sought for with a curious eye.

Ancient Rome, like any modern city, had many prostitutes from whom sex could be bought, and most middle and upper class families had slave girls, whose favours could be had for free. Ovid, however, had no interest in buying sex; it was, he knew, both emotionally unsatisfying and degrading for both parties.

Hence if you wish to find a 'worthy' woman, he says you must go to the right places, where such women gather. In Ovid's Rome the best places to meet attractive, educated women were the trendy streets and walkways, certain temples (especially those dedicated to Venus and Isis), the chariot-racing and horse-racing arenas, and, best of all, the theatres:

The theatres are berries for the fair;
Like ants to mole-hills, thither they repair:
Like bees to hives, so numerously they throng,
It may be said, they to that place belong.
Thither they swarm, who have the public voice;
There choose, if plenty not distract thy choice;
To see, and to be seen, in heaps they run;
Some to undo, and some to be undone.

These days it's much easier to meet the opposite sex.
Men and women work together, and often enjoy themselves in pubs, clubs, discos, parks, and other places.
While theatres may no longer lure young women in quite
the same numbers, you can still get talking to someone
you fancy in a theatre interval. But Ovid's message is
plain: don't sit at home feeling sorry for yourself if you
don't have a girlfriend (or boyfriend) – get out and about
'to see, and to be seen'.

However, before you set foot outside you must make
yourself presentable. For no matter how nice or clever you
are, first impressions count for a great deal. And women,
like men, prefer someone who is attractive to look at,
which in turn suggests that they are attractive inside.
Here is Ovid's advice:

Be not too finical, but yet be clean;
And wear well fashioned clothes like other men.
Let not your teeth be yellow or be foul;
Nor in wide shoes your feet too loosely roll.
Of a black muzzle and long beard beware,
And let a skilful barber cut your hair;
Your nails be pick'd from filth, and even pared;
Nor let your nasty nostrils bud with beard.
Cure your unsav'ry breath, gargle your throat:
And free your arm-pits from the ram and goat.
Dress not, in short, too little or too much:
And be not wholly French, nor wholly Dutch.

The advice about cleaning the fingernails is certainly
something that many modern males should follow. Men

might not notice a woman's hands because they are usually looking at other parts of her, but she will always notice theirs. After all, those hands might one day be caressing her – and if the nails are dirty then she will understandably be put off. Dandruff is also unpleasant, as of course is nose-picking, cleaning out the ears, and yawning without covering your mouth.

Ovid knew that a handsome man always had the initial advantage in matters of love, but said that men of more homely appearance could make themselves attractive by using their other attributes. He mentions Ulysses, who was a short-legged, red-haired, ugly man, but had women falling over themselves to sleep with him. How did he do it? Simply by being a fascinating talker:

> The fam'd Ulysses was not fair or young,
> But eloquent and charming with his tongue;
> And yet for him contending beauties strove,
> And every sea nymph sought the hero's love.

While your appearance is important, it is what you say that will arouse a woman's interest. This is why Ovid suggests that all would-be lovers improve their minds and educate themselves. However good-looking you may be, no woman is going to fancy a man who has nothing but beer, football and cars in his head. The remedy lies in reading more widely to learn a little about a lot, and developing a good sense of humour.

So let's imagine you've sorted out your appearance and honed up on all the hottest topics of conversation. You go into a pub full of single women. But how do you make contact with the one you fancy?

Our friend Ovid favours the direct approach, which can work quite well if you don't make your intentions too obvious. In the situation he imagines, a man has seen a lovely woman at a chariot race, and is urged not to hesitate:

But boldly next the fair your seat provide;
Close as you can to hers, and side by side.
Pleas'd or displeas'd no matter; crowding sit:
For so the laws of public shows permit,
Then find occasion to begin discourse;
Inquire whose chariot this, and whose that horse.
To whatsoever side she is inclin'd,
Suit all your inclinations to her mind;
Like what she likes, from thence your court begin;
And whom she favours, wish that he may win.

A seated woman is, in general, an easier target than one who is standing, as it is harder for her to move away. But anyway, why should she? You are perfectly entitled, as Ovid says, to sit next to her or near her in a public place. Having done that, you should immediately ask her for some information (in exactly the same way that you would ask another man), and agree with her if she expresses any opinion or preference.

This is obviously easier if you are at an event like a horse race or a motorcycle race, where you are both watching the runners or riders, but with a little imagination the same technique can be used anywhere. After all, there's always the weather to talk about, or some local happening, or something interesting in the news. Don't express contrary opinions and don't argue with her, however pleasantly, or you will lessen your chances. You must present yourself as a man who is mentally in tune with her and who thinks she has something interesting to say. Women are always complaining that men never listen to them or take them seriously. You need to show her that you are not like that.

Once you have started your neutral chat and have gained her attention, the next step is to make some equally neutral physical contact:

If dust be on her lap, or grains of sand,
Brush both away with your officious hand.
If there be none, yet brush that nothing hence;

And still to touch her lap make some pretence.
Touch anything of hers . . .

At the same time you should smile a lot and make eye contact as often as possible. If she cracks a joke, make sure you laugh even if it isn't very funny. And if she asks you anything, give a plausible-sounding answer. The important thing is to come over as agreeable and confident:

If she enquires the name of conquer'd kings,
Of mountains, rivers, and their hidden springs,
Answer to all thou know'st; and if need be,
Of things unknown seem to speak knowingly . . .
Talk probably, no matter for the truth.

Ovid appreciated that drinking helped people loosen up, making them laugh and feel friendly. But he warns against drinking too much, especially when you have only just met, as you have to keep your wits about you. So drink in moderation, but make sure that you buy her a drink when her glass is empty, and one for any girlfriend she might be with.

It's important to be nice to her girlfriend too, because they will talk about you later and you want her friend to express a favourable opinion of you. So make her girlfriend your friend as quickly as you can. And by doing so, you will gain her good opinion. And you will also profit from the possible rivalry the girlfriend might present to the woman you really want. Her interest in you will be heightened by the slight sense of competition.

You are now in a position to press ahead with your attack, remembering that:

All women are content that men should woo
She who complains, and she who will not do.
Rest then secure, whate'er thy luck may prove,
Not to be hated for declaring love.

The woman will be flattered by your attention, for all women need to feel that they are attractive to men, and this in itself gives you a psychological advantage. Indeed, you must now take things a step further by flattering her verbally, for it is by flattery, according to Ovid, that women are won:

> By flatteries we prevail on womankind;
> As hollow banks by streams are undermined.
> Tell her, her face is fair, her eyes are sweet;
> Her taper fingers praise, and little feet.
> Such praises e'en the chaste are pleased to hear;
> Both maids and matrons hold their beauty dear.

Such things, if said with apparent – or better still, genuine – honesty, cannot fail to endear you to her. However, if she is not all that lovely, or has obvious flaws in her appearance, you need to cast her inadequacies in a positive light:

> With care conceal whate'er defects you find,
> To all her faults seem like a lover blind . . .
> If pale and meagre, praise her shape and youth,
> Active, when small; when gross, she's plump and smooth.
> Every excess by softening terms disguise,
> And in some neighb'ring virtue hide each vice.
> Nor ask her age . . .

Using these tactics will probably get you as far as walking her home or arranging a date. If so, you will have cleared the first hurdle in the race to win her heart. Now you need to continue your pursuit, adding to your appeal by giving her inexpensive yet well-chosen presents, and, more importantly, by promising expensive gifts (even if you never mean to buy them):

> With promis'd gifts her easy mind bewitch;
> For e'en the poor in promise may be rich.
> Vain hopes awhile her appetite will stay,

'Tis a deceitful but commodious way.
Who gives is mad; but make her still believe
'Twill come, and that's the cheapest way to give.

It's also a good idea to write to her. Not only will she be touched to receive a letter from you, she will also be able to dwell upon it at leisure. In fact Ovid believed that love affairs are often best begun by letter, because they give the shy and less confident lover a chance to express himself more easily. He recommends:

In a familiar style your thoughts convey;
And write such things at present you would say;
Such words as from the heart may seem to move;
'Twas wit enough to make her think you love . . .

You must continue to be both charming and agreeable, and if you have talents, such as being able to dance well or play the guitar, don't hesitate to display them. Flattery will always be your most effective tactic, although Ovid warns:

Be cautious lest you overact your part,
And temper your hypocrisy with art;
Let no false actions give your words the lie,
For once deceiv'd, she's ever after shy.

You will know you are approaching the winning post when you get your first kiss:

If once she kiss, her meaning is express'd;
There wants but little pushing for the rest.

If this is how a male lover should proceed, what advice does Ovid have for a woman who wants to get her man? Our poet knew that women generally have the advantage, as they tend to be the pursued rather than the pursuers. But, on the other hand, they sometimes have to cope with

men's infidelity. They may also find it harder to attract
and keep a man when their looks start to fade:

> Alas, how soon a clear complexion fades!
> How soon a wrinkled skin plump flesh invades!
> And what avails it, though the fair one swears
> She from her infancy had some grey hairs?
> She grows all hoary in a few more years,
> And then the venerable truth appears.

Ovid naturally recommends that a woman should make
the best of her appearance, although he says you must not
overdo it:

> Too rich a dress may sometimes check desire,
> And cleanliness more animate love's fire.

Your hairstyle should suit the shape of your face, and
you ought to wear colours that harmonize with your
complexion. And of course you must always smell fresh
and fragrant.

With all the advice given in books and magazines about
how to enhance your looks, it's hardly necessary to quote
all Ovid's beauty tips! But it's worth mentioning that he
says you should never let a man see you beautifying
yourself:

> For many things when done afford delight,
> Which yet while doing may offend the sight . . .
> While we suppose you sleep, repair your face,
> Lock'd from observers in some secret place;
> Add the last hand before yourselves you show;
> Your need of art why should your lover know?
> For many things when most conceal'd are best;
> And few of strict inquiry bear the test.

If you have imperfections or defects, as most of us do,
try to avoid drawing attention to them:

Whose fingers are too fat, and nails too coarse,
Should always shun much gesture in discourse.
And you whose breath is touch'd, this caution take,
Nor fasting, nor too near another speak.
Let not the nymph with laughter much abound,
Whose teeth are black, uneven, or unsound.
You'd hardly think how much on this depends,
And how a laugh it spoils a face or mends.
Gape not too wide lest you disclose your gums,
And lose the dimple which the cheek becomes . . .
Neglect no means which may promote your ends;
Now learn what way of walking recommends.
Too masculine a motion shocks the sight;
But female grace allures with strange delight.

Ovid further suggests that you should learn to sing well. He argues that a pleasant voice can touch the heart and will more than make up for any lack of beauty. More practically, from a modern point of view, he says you must learn to dance. This will enable you to catch men's eyes and mingle with them on the dance floor. Read love poetry too, he advises, as amorous writing will help put you in the mood for love. And he also recommends that you learn how to play games, including chess, saying:

Learn ev'ry game, you'll find it prove of use;
Parties begun at play, may love produce.

As you cannot meet a man by staying at home, you must of course get out and visit likely places, especially those where men gather in large numbers. The more men there are, the better chance you have of coming across one you fancy and who fancies you:

A hungry wolf at all the herd will run,
In hopes through many to make sure of one.
So let the fair [i.e. you] the gazing crowd assail,
That over one, at least she may prevail.
In every place to please, be all her thought;
Where sometimes least we think, the fish is caught.

You must, however, take care to avoid those men who are too smartly or neatly dressed, as Ovid claims they are bound to be bores; those who are too elaborately dressed, as they are likely to be effeminate; and those who are too expensively dressed, as they may be conmen.

As far as age is concerned, Ovid recommends older men rather than younger ones. This, he says, is because older men are not only more mature, but are also likely to be more sexually experienced, and hence more satisfying in bed. Young men, according to Ovid, tend to be jealous, excitable, argumentative and aggressive, and are less likely to appreciate you. However, as Ovid was 42 when he wrote this, one can't help thinking that he had his own interests at heart!

When you first meet a man, you should give him the impression that he is the only one in your life, which will make him feel special. But as time goes by it's better if he feels a little less secure. A bit of anxiety about possible rivals will stop him becoming complacent and will keep his interest on the boil:

> When first a lover you design to charm,
> Beware lest jealousies his soul alarm;
> Make him believe, with all the skill you can,
> That he and only he's the happy man.
> Anon, by due degrees small doubts create,
> And let him fear some rival's better fate.
> Such little arts make love its vigour hold,
> Which else would languish and too soon grow old.

Pretty soon your chosen man will want to get you into bed. But Ovid says you are a fool if you give in to him straight away; rather, let him wait for his desires to be satisfied:

> Who yields too soon will soon her lover lose;
> Would you retain him long? then long refuse.

The poet suggests dining by candlelight, as its glow will enhance your looks, and says wine will add to the romantic ambience. But he warns against drinking too much wine yourself, saying:

> It warms the blood, adds lustre to the eyes,
> And wine and love have always been allies.
> But carefully from all intemp'rance keep,
> Nor drink till you see double, lisp, or sleep;
> For in such sleeps brutalities are done,
> Which though you loath, you have no power to shun.

We must now bid adieu to Ovid and go on to examine some more recently discovered secrets of love. But do remember that what the poet says is still valid today. Whether male or female, you are far more likely to gain success in love if you take note of his advice.

Sadly, Ovid's own dearest wish – that he should die while making love – was not granted by the goddess he had served so long:

> May Venus grant me but my last desire,
> In the full height of rapture to expire.
> Perhaps some friend, with kindly dew supply'd,
> Weeping will say, 'as Ovid lived, he died'.

In fact, he died alone in bed, far from his beloved Rome.

Chapter 4
SEXUAL SIGNALS

Every hour is lost, which is not spent in love.
                              Lucilio Vanini (1585–1619)

We are seldom direct in what we say when we first meet someone we find attractive. Only the rash will blurt out, 'I think you're lovely, why don't we go out together?'

There are two reasons for this. First, we rarely decide to go out with someone because of looks alone. We need to hear them speak and to get some idea of their personality before taking things further. After all, we have all met people who, while attractive to look at, have voices or attitudes that put us right off them. Second, we all have fragile egos and we fear rejection. So we want to be fairly sure of their answer before we ask them out. Obviously, if we think it will be no, we won't ask them, but if we believe it might be yes, we will.

Despite the advances in sexual equality due to the feminist movement, it is still usually men who have to make the first move. This is why it is so important for them to be able to 'read' the signals that women give out, while women need to know that they are giving out the right ones.

These signals or messages are really just small body movements or, in some cases, lack of movement, which reveal how we feel about someone. They are usually made unconsciously, and are often very subtle. This can be an advantage: if our messages are ignored, we can easily pretend we were just being friendly, thus avoiding embarrassment.

Unfortunately, most men find it difficult to read body signals because they tend to be less intuitive than women and have been brought up to think logically and communicate verbally. A woman is generally far better at working out whether a man is interested in her, but is often frustrated by his apparent blindness to the clues she is giving him. Indeed, the man who is successful with women often owes his success, not to his striking looks or personality, but to the fact that he 'knows' which ones fancy him. In other words, he can interpret their sexual signals.

LOOKING AND SMILING

The first and most important clue is in the eyes. If we look at someone with interest, they will eventually glance back, so establishing eye contact. If she (or he) likes what they see, the glance will be held for slightly longer than if they do not. And just as important, it will be repeated fairly quickly, as they check to see if you are still looking at them. This enables them to establish that your look was really an interested one.

There is a difference, however, between looking and staring. A stare is an unblinking gaze, which has an aggressive edge to it. It may be given by men who regard women as inferior beings, who are only there for their sexual gratification. Or a stare might be given by a man who would like to approach the woman but knows he cannot, because he is married or too unattractive, which makes him angry with himself and her. Being stared at makes most people feel very uncomfortable. And if the stare is accompanied by blank facial features, it is even more off-putting.

A look, by contrast, is given more hesitatingly. It involves blinking, and the face always has an expression that suggests warmth. Indeed, the second or third time a couple make eye contact, they will invariably smile at each other, briefly and tentatively perhaps, yet there will be sufficient movement of the mouth to show that they have each understood the meaning of the other one's look.

However, it is usually the woman who smiles first, the male smile being a rapid response to hers. This happens because women always smile more easily than men. They also know that if a man is looking at them, he is interested, hence a smile on their part is likely to get a response. The male slowness in smiling is due to their fear that they might not get a response, which would leave them feeling rejected. In fact the admiring man is sometimes so surprised by the woman's smile that he is too shocked to return it, although he will invariably do so the next time their eyes meet, having been given the confidence he needs. Later looks are usually partnered by longer and more intense smiles, which of course reinforce their meaning. Indeed, it is no exaggeration to say that looking and smiling are the two most important signals a man and woman can exchange.

But we also look and smile at each other when we are simply being friendly. How then do you tell the difference between a friendly look and smile and an amorous look and smile? The difference lies in the circumstances and in the intensity of the smiles and the length and frequency of the looks.

If a couple are looking at one another from a distance – perhaps on opposite sides of a coffee bar – there can be no mistaking the amorous meaning of their glances and smiles. But if the same pair are at a party, where looks and smiles are being exchanged by everyone, more caution is required. Then you have to judge the other person's interest in you by how often he (or she) looks at you and smiles. If the glances are frequent, even if they are only brief, it shows that he is more interested in you than in anyone else.

The smiles will also be different. Friendly smiles are usually full smiles, with no hint of trepidation about them. Such full, friendly smiles will be given to everyone. An amorous smile, by contrast, is always thinner and less obvious, becoming fuller only later when the person is quite sure of your interest. Hence if the person you fancy looks at you more often than at others in the group, and accompanies such glances with more secretive smiles, you can be sure they like the look of you and would welcome an approach.

Another important clue is in the eyes. Normally when the light brightens, the pupils contract; when it dims, they enlarge. If you are close enough to the person to check his pupils, you should be able to see them enlarging when he looks at you. This is an entirely unconscious reaction; it tells you that he is very taken by what he sees. In fact he will probably notice a similar change in the size of your pupils.

This is such a powerful sign of interest that women used to put an infusion of the juice of deadly nightshade (*atropa bella-donna*) into their eyes to make the pupils enlarge. This accounts for the species name *bella-donna* ('beautiful lady'). It is also the reason why candlelit dinners are considered to be so romantic, as the flickering candlelight not only makes the eyes sparkle, it also brings about a natural enlargement of the pupils. (Flushed cheeks, another sign of excitement, were once created by taking a hot bath and then washing the face in white wine. Try it some time!)

A person who is interested in you will hold your gaze for slightly longer than normal. But you should also notice where else their glances are directed – at your mouth, your hair, your hands, or even at more intimate parts of you. This is all part of a more general 'checking you out' routine. Such glances are often accompanied by parted lips, which in itself suggests sexual attraction and a willingness to open up to you.

GETTING CLOSER

These signals should be enough to tell you *when* to make your move but you still have to work out *how*. If you have exchanged glances and smiles in a coffee bar, for example, you might use going up to pay the bill as a way of getting physically closer and finding an opportunity to talk to each other.

At a party or dance, where people are standing and moving about, making an approach is obviously easier and less likely to cause embarrassment. In fact in such a situation both of you might gradually edge closer to one another, perhaps while talking to other people, until, without seeming to pick each other out, you are able to begin your own conversation.

If you are still not sure whether the person genuinely fancies you, take note of how close they stand. Each of us likes to keep an invisible body space around us. Only those who are emotionally important to us are allowed to enter this space. We try to keep strangers a certain distance from us, by moving away from them if necessary.

When two people are standing talking to one another they always keep a distance of at least 2 feet between them, even if they know each other. So if the person moves closer to you, not only do they want to enter your body space, but you are being allowed into theirs. It is a signal that you are more important than anyone else. If you are at a crowded party you may actually be pressed up against one another, but such artificial closeness cannot be so clearly interpreted as when it happens out of choice.

Physical closeness not only allows you to talk to each other, it also gives you both a chance to carry out a more personal inspection. A person's acne scars or bad breath may not have been noticeable at a distance but will become all too apparent at close quarters. If the effect is really off-putting, you or the other person will probably move away, with averted eyes and a tight, regretful smile.

But if you both pass the close personal inspection, then the simple physical proximity of your bodies acts as another powerful signal. For one thing it brings into play your personal odours.

Your breath and skin contain natural substances called pheromones which help to create sexual excitement. Perfume or aftershave may add to your allure but don't douse yourself with them to such an extent that you drown out your natural – and far sexier – smells. These natural odours are of course appreciated most intensely when a couple embrace, particularly when they are naked, as it is then that the pheromones play their full part in sexual arousal.

So you're standing close together, looking into each other's eyes. You can see the other person's enlarged pupils, which say 'I'm interested', and gazing at each other focuses your attention, effectively cutting you off from what's going on around you. Your closeness and self-absorption also tell other people that you have, at least temporarily, committed yourselves to one another.

BODY LANGUAGE

In such a situation, both you and the other person will adopt an 'open' body posture, standing directly facing one another, with unfolded arms. Folding our arms is one of the ways we isolate ourselves from others, the arms forming a physical barrier between us and them. Unfolding the arms, by contrast, indicates that we are open to the other person. This body openness may be emphasized by the man undoing his jacket, or by the woman perhaps moving a handbag that she had held across her stomach to one side.

During this period, if not before, conversation will have started between you, giving you both the opportunity to hear each other's voice and also to pick up clues about each other's personality. While talking enables you to exchange information, it also allows you to react to each other, by smiling, laughing, frowning, and so on. The face looking at you then becomes attractive not simply because of its features, but because its emotional reactions are dancing in tune with your own.

The next sign to watch out for is touching. Touching never takes place accidentally, unless of course you and the other person are pushed together. Invariably it involves one of you deliberately touching some part of the other person's body. At first the man may just take hold of the woman's elbow to move her out of somebody else's way, or the woman might brush cigarette ash from the man's lapel. More often, though, the touch will give apparent emphasis to some point made during conversation. Or when the couple laugh, the woman will drop a hand on to one of the man's hands, or on to his arm, or even – and this only happens when the couple are sitting – on to his leg.

The first touch is brief – the hand is quickly withdrawn – but it will be followed by touches that last fractionally longer, especially if they are returned by the man. It is the woman who normally begins such touching, which in itself shows that she would like her touching to lead to a greater physical closeness, perhaps even an embrace.

Closely linked to touching is 'mirroring', whereby you both start to imitate the other's actions. You may both, for example, light a cigarette at the same time, or drink at the same time, or mimic one another's body postures. If you form part of a larger group, you may nod your heads together in agreement, or shake them in disapproval, or laugh together. Such mirroring demonstrates that you have become, in effect, a couple, united by your interest in one another and by the hope of further involvement. In fact by this time, you will probably have decided to leave the club or party together, or if that is not possible, you will have exchanged phone numbers or arranged to meet again.

MAKING CONVERSATION

What is said by a couple meeting for the first time, when neither one is entirely relaxed, is perhaps less important than *how* it is said. Both will actually be listening to the sound of the other's voice, to his or her accent, and to how the words are expressed. Women expect a man's voice to have a masculine depth to it; whereas men might find a husky female voice sexy but they don't want her to sound too masculine.

Each will also be watching to see how the other one smiles as they speak, because this gives an insight into the warmth of his or her personality. Warmth of manner is very important because it tends to go with kindness, friendliness and the ability to love. Indeed, when interviewed about what they look for in a partner, most people place kindness and intelligence higher than good looks. So if you want to make a favourable impression, don't go on about bringing back the death penalty or your passion for fox-hunting!

In general, men tend to be more interested in how a woman looks than in what she has to say or her social status. Women, on the other hand, usually pay more attention to what a man says about himself, even though he may be lying through his teeth. Many women want to know if a man will make a stable and successful long-term partner, so it is in their interest to find out what he does for a living, the position he occupies, and what his ambitions are. This does not mean they are uninterested in sex, simply that they don't normally think only of sex.

However, women often find certain men sexy and desirable, who, judged on their looks alone, could never be so described. These lucky few are made desirable by their glamorous professions. They might be rock stars, actors, photographers, writers, or perhaps they participate in some hazardous sport like parachuting, surfing, motor-racing, or playing rugby or polo. Such men can occasionally be interesting in themselves, but all too often they turn out to be boring and arrogant.

However, many men have jobs that, while unglamorous, give them a good income and a secure future, such as banking, accounting, computing, and so on. Not surprisingly, when meeting a woman they hope to seduce, they sometimes tell lies in order to seem more interesting. This is not advisable as it is not only morally wrong but you will sooner or later be found out, and few things will put a woman off faster than dishonesty.

While many women would like a man with a glamorous occupation, this will not matter at all once they have fallen in love with you. Indeed, a woman in love will excuse anything, even the misfortune of being an accountant! What you need to do is make sure that she's too smitten to care by the time she finds out what it is you actually do for a living. Simply steer the conversation away from your work and concentrate on telling her how lovely she is. Women, as Ovid noted, love to be complimented, so tell her how much you admire her blue eyes, her cute snub nose, her hairstyle, her fabulous figure, and anything else you can think of. Even attractive women are often insecure about their looks, and love to hear themselves praised, especially by a man they fancy. So flatter, but do it with conviction.

You must also remember that women like talking to men. So listen to what she says, agree with what she says, and laugh at any jokes she tells. Give the impression that you find her conversation totally absorbing, even if it isn't. Whatever you do, don't make the mistake of hogging the conversation yourself, except when you flatter her. Most men don't converse, they monopolize, talking endlessly about themselves and how wonderful they are. If you do this you will either give too much away or have her fleeing from you out of boredom, to find someone else who is less tiresome.

It's always good to laugh together. A mutual laugh will strengthen the bond between you and, perhaps just as importantly, help to relax you. But having a sense of humour is not the same as telling a string of dirty jokes, which is what many men tend to do. Few women like listening to an endless stream of dirty jokes. In fact men who do this will not be judged amusing, but dull and dirty-minded.

Humour can often spring from the subject being spoken about, from incongruities, from unusual observations or from wordplay, and the best humour is subtle not vulgar. Hence men should try to be pleasantly humorous, but if this type of humour is beyond you, then don't try to be funny at all; let the woman crack the jokes instead and you provide the laughter. Laughter from you will reward her and will further endear you to her. Keep in mind that a sense of humour is one of the qualities that both sexes most desire in a partner. Your laughter will show that you can see the funny side of things.

Again, if you are a woman, you will help yourself by fixing your attention on the man you're with. Don't try to capture him and play the coquette with other men at the same time. You should avoid gazing around, checking out other men and perhaps even smiling at them, even though you may do this in a seemingly innocent and friendly way. The man you're with will prefer you to ignore the opposition and concentrate exclusively on him. Any man is attracted to a woman who is available to him but not to anyone else, because this makes him seem irresistible.

SLEEPING TOGETHER

Although men are always hoping to have sex sooner rather than later, they seldom respect women who sleep with them too quickly. They might not put it in so many words, but they often think the woman will jump into bed with someone else just as easily. This makes them scared of being cheated on and makes it difficult for them to trust their partner. Any long-term relationship is based on mutual trust. When that is lost, the relationship effectively ends, and if it was never there, the relationship can never become anything more than exploitation.

This is why the advice offered to women by Ovid almost 2,000 years ago is still true today and is worth repeating:

Who yields too soon will soon her lover lose;
Would you retain him long? then long refuse.

Nothing in life that is gained easily, whether it be sex or anything else, is valued very highly. So, even if a man professes undying love for you, don't sleep with him too soon, however attractive he is. By waiting, you give him the message that you consider yourself worth waiting for. In other words, when you do make love it will be a truly special experience for you both, not a throwaway fling that hardly matters. He will also feel that he has 'earned' something, and that you in turn have 'given' him something worth having. Your lovemaking will at that point help to strengthen your relationship, giving it a chance to become a long-standing one and not merely a brief encounter.

How soon you sleep with a man depends on several things. If he is always trying to get you into bed, then he obviously only wants you for sex, and, once satisfied, he will probably start backing away from you. He may even drop you there and then. Such a man should be avoided. If, by contrast, he is quite happy to take you out or be with you without always having sex on his mind, he probably hopes for more than a purely sexual relationship. If you have strong religious or moral principles, you may decide to make him wait until your wedding night. Otherwise you'll know when the time is right for both of you.

Finally, don't fall into the trap of thinking that if you don't have sex with a man he will leave you for someone else. He might, but ask yourself: if he's really attracted to you as a person, won't he respect your wishes? If he doesn't, it means he's only interested in sex, he doesn't deserve you anyway, and you're better off without him.

Chapter 5
BODY MESSAGES

Our bodies reveal a great deal about us. Our mood, our personality, our sexual and romantic nature are all reflected in the way we dress, move, eat, speak and laugh. Learning to read these body messages should help you on the path to success in love.

EYES

We always look at someone's eyes when we are interested in them as a possible lover. Eye colour and eye movement give out some of our most important body messages.

Research has shown that people with either brown or blue eyes (the most common colours among Europeans) stand at opposite ends of a personality spectrum. Those with brown eyes tend to have quick reactions and make rapid decisions. They are rather impatient, have a lot of energy, and are also somewhat short-tempered. Hence brown-eyed people like to be out and about. They function best when the problem they are tackling is easily and speedily dealt with. They are not suited to the long haul and they dislike deviousness, dishonesty and a calculating nature. They prefer to put their cards on the table.

Blue-eyed people are usually quite different. Their eye colour is linked with a more serious, introspective and thoughtful manner. The blue-eyed hate making quick decisions; they like to consider all the possibilities before making up their minds. They may seem less energetic than their brown-eyed cousins, yet they are good at solving long-term problems. In fact they prefer to plan ahead and work towards distant goals instead of hoping for early success. They are introverts by nature, whereas brown-eyed people are more likely to be extroverts. Blue-eyed people behave in a colder, more calculating way than the brown-eyed. They prefer to keep their cards close to their chests.

But while these character traits usually apply in general, you also need to consider the actual shade of the eye colour. Those with light-coloured brown eyes will be less excitable and more thoughtful than the dark brown-eyed, in the same way that those with dark blue eyes will be warmer and less calculating than those with light blue eyes. Indeed, people with washed-out 'American movie star' blue eyes tend to be very unemotional.

The hazel-eyed fall somewhere in the middle. They are warmer and more outgoing than the average blue-eyed person, yet have greater staying power and are less excitable than the average brown-eyed person. In other words, they are emotionally stable, yet capable of dealing with change and new ideas. For this reason they tend to be happier with themselves and their achievements than either the brown-eyed or the blue-eyed.

Grey-eyed people have much in common with the blue-eyed, in that they tend to be thinkers and dislike being rushed. They are suspicious of their emotions, which they like to keep under control. Green-eyed people are perhaps the most individual of all the eye colour types, and are reputed to be clever, cheerful, inventive and charming.

A knowledge of the personality traits associated with a particular eye colour can help you make the right sort of approach. For example, a fun-loving, outgoing brown-eyed person will prefer a direct, open approach, whereas the blue-eyed will respond to one that is slower and more considered.

Similarly, if someone with blue eyes makes a pass at you, you can be pretty sure that he (or she) has been planning to do so for a while, unlike a brown-eyed person who is more likely to approach you on impulse. And because the blue-eyed person is persistent, he or she may not take no for an answer, while if you play hard to get with brown-eyed people they might just try their luck elsewhere.

You can also expect a date with a brown-eyed person to be more interesting and probably more fun than one with a blue-eyed person, although this partly depends on your own personality. If you are blue-eyed, you may prefer the laid-back style of another blue-eyed person to a more frantic and disorganized brown-eyed partner. The brown-eyed person will certainly be more open to suggestions. The blue-eyed man or woman will want to stick to what they have planned, and they don't like surprises anyway.

Because the brown-eyed tend to be more irritable and short-tempered than blue-eyed people, you may have more disagreements, although the upsets will blow over quickly. Blue-eyed people are calmer in mood and slow to anger, but watch out for the fireworks when they do get mad – and don't expect them to quickly forgive and forget. Blue-eyed people tend to think before they act. They are only violent when they are driven to it, whereas the brown-eyed are usually more forceful.

Eye movement is also important. If their pupils don't increase in size when they first look at you, they will probably have difficulty in becoming emotionally involved with you, even if they say otherwise. But pupil enlargement is only a sign of interest in the early stages of a relationship. You don't need to worry if it fails to occur later on.

Ideally your partner's eyes should be bright and set on the same level. The whites should be white (rather than yellowish) without visible blood vessels. And you should not be able to see any white either above or below the irises when they are looking straight ahead. Eyes like these symbolize a bright, alert personality, emotional stability, and an honest, open character. They also signify success for their owner between the ages of 34 and 39, which is the life period covered by the eyes.

Some people's irises 'float' too high, so that the white of the eye is visible between them and the lower eyelids (see Figure 31). This feature is called *sanpaku* by Oriental experts, who claim that it signifies emotional instability and negative, destructive tendencies, which can result in angry outbursts and even physical violence.

Figure 31 Irises 'floating' too high.

Irises that sink too low, so that the white of the eyes appears above them, another type of *sanpaku*, can betoken a cruel and emotionally abnormal psychological type (see Figure 32).

Figure 32 Irises 'sinking' too low.

When bright eyes are partnered by a steady, direct gaze they are commonly described as 'masterful'. Those with masterful eyes tend to rise to the highest positions. So if you become involved with someone who has masterful eyes, they will have a lot of self-confidence and will also possess (if the eyes are accompanied by strong, balanced features) qualities such as drive, energy, patience and perseverance, which will help them achieve their ambitions. But do remember that such people may spend much time advancing their careers at the expense of their relationships.

Dull eyes symbolize a lack of alertness and spontaneity, and eyes which dart about here and there indicate an absence of drive and persistence. When combined, they mark out a person who is unlikely to achieve much in life. Such people will prove disappointing to themselves and to you.

CLOTHES

You can also gain clues to someone's personality and availability from the way they dress. In general, those who are married or involved in a relationship keep more of their bodies concealed than those who are unattached. Our clothes can of course accentuate all the curves and bulges that attract the opposite sex. Single women, for example, often wear bras that give maximum uplift. They may draw further attention to their breasts by wearing tight blouses, sweaters or low-cut tops. Hips and buttocks can be similarly emphasized with tight jeans or skirts.

Attached women, by contrast, tend to downplay their sexuality with looser and less revealing clothing. Their blouses are usually buttoned up and their skirts are often longer. Such increased modesty in dress is matched by less striking make-up and jewellery, and perhaps by a more conservative hairstyle.

In a similar way, men who are single and unattached try to emphasize their broad shoulders, big chests and bulging crotches by wearing padded jackets, tight T-shirts or sweaters and tight jeans. Shirts will frequently be left unbuttoned to reveal some chest hair and the sleeves may be rolled up to show the naked arms and biceps (if any). Ties are seldom worn.

When the same man has settled down with a woman he usually starts to dress more conservatively. T-shirts tend to be avoided, shirts are buttoned up higher or worn with a tie, and jeans or trousers are chosen to be comfortable rather than crotch-hugging. Indeed, a woman may be well advised to keep an eye on what her mate chooses to wear when he goes out alone. If he continues to favour revealing clothing, or if he starts to dress more like a single man, the chances are that he's not as committed as he might pretend. And the relationship is likely to be in serious trouble if he starts jogging or lifting weights!

Both the clothing style and the colours worn send out useful messages. Arty, independent-minded people usually choose a very unusual, individual style. However, this can sometimes be nothing more than a pose. Although they want to appear more interesting, and thereby more desirable, to the opposite sex, they are often rather untalented, ordinary people, who hope that a bizarre appearance will cover up their poor self-image and sense of inadequacy.

The colours worn by attention-seeking people are invariably bright, eye-catching ones like red and orange. Black is popular with the person who wants to be regarded as sophisticated and mysterious, whereas white – suggesting coolness and aloofness – is often worn by someone who is warm underneath, yet shy.

Dr Max Luscher, the Swiss researcher who devised a colour test for determining personality, claims that our choice of colours is unconscious, as is our reaction to them. Those who wear red, he says, are looking for sexual excitement, and those who wear orange are not averse to lovemaking either. The violet-clad are interested in both spirituality and sexuality, which is why the colour is often favoured by Eastern cults that mix meditation with sex. The wearer of yellow is eager for contact with others and is similarly interested in sex, but unwilling to commit themselves to a partner.

Less striking colours like blue, brown and green are

typically preferred by those who are not seeking attention and whose sexuality is less rampant. They are also calmer and more conventional. Blue symbolizes coolness and peace, and is often favoured by those with strong religious beliefs. Brown signifies calmness, resignation and a love of the home, while green betokens inner stability, harmony and a desire for steady progress through life.

All these psychological associations are modified by the shade of the colour. Some shades, such as electric blue and green, are very eye-catching and denote a more up-tempo and excitable personality. Thus the duller the shade, the more introverted the wearer and the less likely they are to be searching for romance.

Be warned that those who wear brown tend to be pessimistic, and are prone to depression, and that the person clad in black can be insecure. Wearers of brown and black are quite vulnerable emotionally and should be handled with caution and sensitivity.

You must of course take into account the amount of any single colour that a person is wearing, while disregarding those colours that form part of a uniform which they are obliged to wear. For example, a woman who has on a red coat is likely to be far more sexually obsessed than one wearing a red scarf, who may be interested in nothing more than a harmless flirtation. But sexual availability is often indicated by bright red lipstick and nail varnish.

MOVEMENT AND POSTURE

The confident, self-assured person invariably stands upright with his shoulders back, and walks with a bounce, taking long strides and swinging his arms. Such a walking style denotes a good self-image, a basically happy disposition and an ambitious nature. Those who fell less sure of themselves and who are pessimistic about their potential usually have a bowed head and slumped-forward shoulders. They tend to walk with shorter strides and a choppy motion, and may hardly swing their arms at all. Hardly surprisingly, people who are angry or unhappy or depressed also walk like this.

If you have a chance, watch the person you fancy in company. Do they often touch other people? Or do they seem reluctant to do so? Touching is a form of communication, and those who touch others are generally warmer and more emotionally open than those who avoid physical contact. Emotionally inhibited people may not even like shaking hands. Their handshake is brief and often incomplete; or they only offer their fingers to be shaken instead of their whole hand.

The way people hold their arms and legs, or position their hands and bodies, can give an insight into how they are reacting to you. For instance, if you are trying to chat someone up, watch how they position their legs. If they are uncrossed it shows that the person is still undecided about you but open to your approaches. If they cross the leg nearest to you over the other one, so that the nearest knee is directed away from you, they are probably not interested in you and do not wish to be seen with you. However, should they cross the far leg over the one closest to you, thereby directing its knee towards you, then you can be fairly sure that you are making a favourable impression.

Interest is also indicated by the person turning the upper part of their body towards you, even if the twist is slight. If they don't turn towards you, or even turn away from you, your conversation is almost certainly falling on deaf ears.

Likewise, if their arms are folded to form a protective barrier, it reveals a lack of interest – a message that is doubly emphasized if the nearest leg is crossed over the other. As mentioned in the previous chapter, unfolded arms signify openness. And if they move one of their hands towards you, perhaps pushing it along the table in your direction, your chances are good. If that hand drops

– accidentally on purpose – on to your leg or hand, you can be pretty certain of success.

When sitting opposite the person you can gauge their interest by the way they hold their body. Leaning towards you shows they're interested, whereas leaning away usually means they're not. Couples who are angry with each other tend to 'distance' themselves in the same way.

Also, watch their hands. If they keep them out of sight they have no feeling for you, whereas it shows a desire to be close to you if they push their hands or personal possessions towards you, particularly if they push them across a table into 'your half' of it. At the same time, the more eye contact you make, and the more smiles you exchange, the safer you are in assuming that they are happy with you.

Personal possessions can be helpful in other ways. For instance someone you find attractive might visit your home and leave something behind. This is usually something small, like a lighter or a bracelet. Their seeming forgetfulness gives them an excuse to come back, not simply to collect the 'forgotten' object, but to see you. Don't miss the opportunity to show your interest when they turn up.

Chapter 6
MAKING LOVE HAPPEN

Once you've met someone you fancy, is it possible to make them fall in love with you? Or must you simply allow nature to take its course and wait to see what happens?

You may both have fallen in love at first sight. But it's more likely that Cupid, while attracting your attention to one another, will not immediately shoot an arrow into either of your hearts.

Scientists have been trying to discover what exactly makes us fall in love. They haven't reached any conclusions as yet but they all agree that we are responding to certain signals that the loved one gives out. By giving out these signals as soon as you can, you will evoke a loving response in that person. This may seem a rather cold-blooded, calculating thing to do, but 'all's fair in love and war'. And anyway you know you're a worthwhile and lovable person, so why shouldn't you give Cupid's arrow a little help in finding its mark?

First and foremost, you need to make sure that the object of your affection is worth all this effort. They may be good-looking and charming, but you need to know much more about them before you try to capture their heart – or give them yours in return.

Rule number one is 'all that glisters is not gold'. Look at what really lies beneath the surface gloss and don't trust your first impressions. They may be as wonderful as they seem, or they may just be good at turning on the charm.

The second rule is: don't sleep together straight away.

As I explained earlier, making love for the first time should be an experience you build up to, not a meaningless, throwaway one.

You should therefore go out together at least a few times before having sex. This will not only enable you to get to know him (or her) better, but will also give you a chance to follow some of the love tips mentioned below – just as soon, that is, as you've made sure he or she is worth it.

Although nobody is perfect, some qualities are more important than others. Before getting involved any further, you need to find out whether he (or she) is honest, dependable, responsible, and careful with money. If the person has all these traits, you can at least be certain that you won't be lied to, that they will turn up when they say they will, that they won't be neglectful or do stupid things, and that they won't start borrowing money from you. It is not worth the hurt you will suffer if you take up with someone who has any of these faults. And if you don't believe me, ask any of your friends who have been involved with someone who does.

Where honesty is concerned, listen carefully to what he (or she) tells you. The dishonest person always exaggerates – i.e. lies – about his background, his abilities and his achievements. So if what he says about himself sounds improbable, it probably is. And watch out for inconsistencies. It's a good idea to ask him to repeat some seemingly wild tale. If you get essentially the same story the second time around, it's probably true; but if the 'facts' come out differently, then's he's obviously lying, either wholly or in part.

Whenever possible, get some independent confirmation of what he's told you from someone who knows him. And pay close attention to his attitudes to honesty. If he seems to think it's all right to take advantage of others, to lie to them and cheat them, sooner or later he will probably do the same to you.

The dependable person will either turn up on time or

will let you know in advance if he (or she) can't make the date you've arranged. It is true that at times we can all be unavoidably held up, but if he is late more than once you can assume that not only will he be late again, but that eventually he won't bother to turn up at all. Give such a person short shrift – don't wait about for a man or woman who keeps you waiting.

The responsible person will either be working or actively looking for a job. He will also have certain commitments. If his parents are alive, he will write to them, telephone them or visit them regularly. If he has a pet or some plants, he will look after them. And if he has things to do, he does them. Dependability and responsibility are two sides of the same coin, and you should find that a man or woman who is dependable is also responsible.

The financially prudent person won't overwhelm you with gifts or spend too freely, but he won't be in debt either. Such a person will be prepared to pay their way. Although the man traditionally used to pay for the woman, now that most women are working there is no reason why they can't buy their share of the drinks and meals. If the person you date asks to borrow money from you (without a *very* good reason), refuse – and refuse to see him again as well. Not only will he probably never repay you, he will almost certainly ask to borrow more. And you can do without that.

Women should watch out for any signs of aggression or violence. If the man you fancy is at all threatening, you can be sure that he will eventually use violence against you, no matter what he might say to the contrary. This is doubly true if he also drinks too much. Macho men are most likely to be violent, because they usually have deep-seated feelings of inadequacy, which they try to cover up by developing a tough-guy image. Unfortunately some women are irresistibly drawn to such men, because their instability gives an exciting, dangerous edge to the relationship. But you will almost certainly live to regret it if you are so tempted. If the man is at all dangerous, or if he drinks too much, drop him and look for someone else.

You should also note how your new boyfriend's or girlfriend's attractiveness compares with your own. Studies have shown that not only are you far more likely to fall in love and marry, but that your union will last for much longer, possibly even for life, if your attractiveness ratings are very similar. In fact the closer you are matched physically and, indeed, intellectually, the better will be your chance of establishing a permanent relationship. Couples who are very different in looks usually only remain together when there is a trade-off, such as when a beautiful woman marries an ugly, but rich and powerful man.

However, men and women react very differently to any inequality in the relationship. 'Women feel extremely uncomfortable if they believe they are getting more than they deserve,' says Dr Elaine Walster, Professor of Psychology and Sociology at the University of Wisconsin, 'whereas they feel pretty comfortable if they think they're being cheated. Men are just the opposite. They're outraged if they're underbenefited, but they're comfortable if they're getting more than they deserve.'

If you think you are both fairly evenly matched physically and intellectually, and if you are pretty sure about your partner's honesty, dependability, responsibility and good financial sense, then you are ready to work at making him or her fall in love with you. It's easier than you might think, particularly if you believe that you are lovable and worth having.

We are most likely to fall in love with people with whom we feel comfortable, and we all feel most comfortable with ourselves. This means that in the early stages of the relationship you should 'mirror' the other person, or make yourself as much like him or her as you can.

In the chapter on 'Sexual Signals' I described how when a couple first meet and are attracted to one another, they spontaneously mirror each other's movements and actions, by drinking at the same time, lighting up cigarettes together, leaning towards one another, and so on. This signals that they are thinking alike and feeling alike. So you need to take this a stage further and mimic, as subtly and unobtrusively as you can, everything about the other person so that he (or she) 'sees' himself in you. In other words, if he feels most comfortable in jeans you should also dress casually; if his favourite shirts are blue, wear blue; if he smokes a particular brand of cigarette, smoke the same brand (if you smoke).

It doesn't hurt to make these changes seemingly because you've been inspired to do so by his tastes. For example, let's say his favourite colour is blue, while yours is black. Start by buying yourself one blue-coloured item such as a blouse, wear it when you go out with him and at some point tell him, 'You look so nice in blue that I decided to buy this blue blouse. I think it suits me. In fact I'm going to wear more blue. It really is an attractive colour.' By saying this and by wearing blue, you not only affirm his taste in colour, but flatter him at the same time. And imitation is the sincerest form of flattery.

At the same time, you can start to imitate him in other ways. Perhaps he's a slow walker, preferring to amble along at an easy pace, whereas you are by nature a brisk walker. When you are out together you should slow down and walk like him. Again, if he speaks slowly in a low-pitched voice, you should try to slow down and lower your voice as far as possible. And if he likes spending time in a pub playing darts, don't just sit there – enter into the spirit of things and enjoy yourself too.

You might object to doing all this on the grounds that you will lose your own personality and tastes in the process. Well, don't worry, you won't – because your behaviour is only a means to an end, which is making him (or her) fall in love with you. Anyway, as time goes by you can start to change back to how you normally dress and behave, while he might start to dress and act slightly differently, under your influence. In other words, you should end up with a compromise that you both feel comfortable with.

If you doubt that mirroring works, have a look at a few happily married couples. Not only do they often look alike, but they are also remarkably similar in the way they dress, what they like to eat and how they eat, and in their general tastes and attitudes. However, mirroring only works successfully if the person likes himself. If he doesn't there is a real danger that he will see everything he dislikes about himself in you. This is why it is so important to make sure that he (or she) has a positive self-image as soon as you can.

You do not need to mention all the changes you make. In fact it is usually better to do things like walking more slowly – without him (or her) being consciously aware of what you're doing, although they will be appreciated at a subconscious level. He (or she) will feel increasingly comfortable with you, and this will soon develop into a *need* to be with you. This emotional attachment is only a short step from being in love with you.

Where attitudes and views are concerned, you should also try to agree with your love target as much as you can. This won't be as difficult as you might think, because if they have a healthy self-image they are unlikely to hold extreme views. By agreeing you flatter him again and thereby emphasize the mirror image you are projecting. Even if some of his opinions are at variance with your own, you will gradually be able to use your increasing influence over him to change his way of thinking. He will listen to alternative ideas more readily because they come from you. But don't start trying to change him until he has fallen in love with you. Until he does, mimic him, agree with him, laugh with him, and generally make him feel entirely comfortable with you.

During this period it's best not to give away too much about yourself. This is particularly true if you have lived an uneventful life. By revealing everything at the start you only underline your ordinariness, whereas you want to remain something of a mystery. So talk about yourself sparingly – letting your partner ask the questions. And show a similar interest in them, as everyone likes to talk about what they've done or plan to do. Caution is likewise required if you have done a great many interesting things. By mentioning too much, too soon you may make them feel inadequate.

Don't always be available to go out on a date, even if you would like to. This will create more interest in you and may add a hint of anxiety that you might be dating someone else. And carry on seeing friends of the opposite sex, making sure that the boyfriend (or girlfriend) sees you talking to them. Remember that a little jealousy helps to heighten interest, fastens the affections and encourages love to grow.

When you go out together, try to do things that neither of you have done before, so that you enjoy such new experiences as a couple. These shared memories will help form a bond between you. But it's best not to go away for weekends together until you have started having sex, otherwise you may feel pressured into sleeping with the person before you feel ready.

Your own feelings for your partner should also deepen during this time. But if they don't you should end the relationship as quickly and amicably as you can. Otherwise they will be very hurt, especially as you will have played an active role in creating their feelings for you.

Sex, of course, will sooner or later come into the picture. You need it to happen at the right time, when he (or she) feels deeply about you, for it can then turn those feelings into love. But you must naturally be guided by your own moral beliefs. If you think sex before marriage is wrong, save yourself for your wedding night. But if you regard pre-marital sex as OK, you should treat it as what it really is, an act of love. Don't allow it to happen in tacky circumstances – like the back of a car – or when it has to be hurried.

You want the first time to be as romantic and as memorable as possible, but remember that you will both be somewhat tense and anxious so don't expect your lovemaking to be utterly ecstatic straight away. If it is, that's wonderful, but if it isn't, tell your lover that you thought it was wonderful anyway. Your real or apparent enjoyment will add to the magic of the moment, relax and encourage your lover, and further tighten the bonds that are forming around his (or her) heart.

Indeed, your lovemaking should ideally be the occasion when he tells you that he loves you and means it, and you him. If so, it will be the moment when you know you have gained his heart.

Chapter 7
Sexual Addiction

Even though an ever-increasing number of marriages end in divorce, most of us still believe in the romantic ideal of meeting someone, falling in love, marrying, and staying together until death us do part. Yet there are those who fear such intimacy, people who want sex without emotional involvement. Such men have traditionally been known as Casanovas, Don Juans, Lotharios, satyrists and priapists, while the women tend to be described as nymphomaniacs. These people have an addictive problem which can be as compulsive and degrading as an addiction to drugs or drink. And there are 'love addicts' as well as 'sex addicts'.

The classic sex addict of literature is Lothario, who appears in a play called *The Fair Penitent*, written by Nicolas Rowe in 1703. In the first act Lothario tells his friend Rossano that he made the beautiful Calista fall in love with him, then entered her bedroom one night and had his way with her. It is worth repeating his words because they describe exactly what happens in the life of a modern sex addict.

Lothario: Hear then, I'll tell thee:
          Once in a lone and secret hour of night,
          When ev'ry eye was clos'd, and the pale moon
          And stars alone shone conscious of the theft,
          Hot with the Tuscan grape, and high in blood,
          Hap'ly I stole unheeded to her chamber.
Rossano: That minute sure was lucky.

Lothario: Oh, 'twas great!
        I found the fond, believing, love-sick maid,
        Loose, unattir'd, warm, tender, full of wishes;
        Fierceness and pride, the guardians of her honour,
        Were charm'd to rest, and love alone was waking.
        Within her rising bosom all was calm,
        As peaceful seas that know no storms, and only
        Are gently lifted up and down by tides.
        I snatch'd the glorious, golden opportunity
        And with prevailing, youthful ardour press'd her,
        'Till with short sighs, and murmuring reluctance,
        The yielding fair-one gave me perfect happiness.
        Ev'n all the live-long night we pass'd in bliss,
        In ecstasies too fierce to last for ever;
        At length, the morn and cold indifference came;
        When, fully sated with the luscious banquet,
        I hastily took leave, and left the nymph
        To think on what was past, and sigh alone.
Rossano: You saw her soon again?
Lothario: Too soon I saw her:
        For, Oh! that meeting was not like the former:
        I found my heart no more beat high with transport,
        No more I sigh'd, and languish'd for enjoyment;
        'Twas past, and reason took her turn to reign,
        While ev'ry weakness fell before her throne.

Once Lothario had possessed Calista he was no longer interested in her. Like a huntsman, he had stalked and taken his quarry. That done, he would soon have been ready to seek fresh prey, and might have done so had not he come to a sticky end.

Not all male sexaholics are turned off as quickly as Lothario, but the relationship seldom lasts very long once they have had sex. For the chase and the possession are more important to them than the sex act itself. In fact psychologists agree that the male sex addict's *raison d'être* is conquest, while for the female it is submission. In other words, they are unable to form a normal loving relationship, but continually seek the thrill of making it with a new partner.

And sex addicts are very good at finding new partners. They know where to look and how to practise the art of seduction. But are they happy people? The answer, as for any addict, is definitely no. Here, for example, is what a 32-year-old Californian insurance salesman, said about his compulsion:

> It gets to the point where you know something is wrong with you – that you can't sleep without it, can't concentrate at work. This urge, it never lets you go. You don't feel good without getting that fix from a woman. And when it's over, you roll over and kind of feel that same awful empty feeling again. And you hate yourself a little.

There are a number of reasons why sex addicts behave as they do, the two most important being a poor self-image and loneliness. Perhaps their parents divorced when they were children, or were too busy to pay them much attention, leaving them with a sense of not being lovable. And sexual abuse in childhood is a common cause of female sexual addiction.

The typical sex addict centres his (or her) life around sex. It is more important than family, job and friends. Such people feel compelled to seek sex and quite powerless to control their behaviour. They also frequently feel lonely, unlovable, guilty and ashamed.

But what is most surprising, according to social worker Vivian Krepak, is that sex addicts don't usually enjoy sex:

> The women are rarely orgasmic, and if they achieve it, it'll take them many hours. It's like there is a bottomless pit. All they want is a real relationship, but feel they don't deserve it or they can't have one. And they conclude that all they have is their body.

The love addict is hooked on being in love and having their love returned, rather than the sex act itself. And because deeper feelings are involved, love addiction can be far more hurtful than an addiction to sex.

Some love addicts flit from one affair to the next, breaking hearts without truly giving their own, while others become fixated on one person. The monogamous love addict may cause trouble if his (or her) beloved tries to end the relationship. He may refuse to believe that it is over, and keep trying to restart the affair, making both himself and the other person more miserable in the process. He may, for example, follow her around, telephone her constantly, insult or even attack her new boyfriend, and generally make a nuisance of himself.

Nigel, a former insurance broker interviewed by Penny Woolcock for her TV documentary 'Falling in Love ... Again', is a love addict of the first type. His love affairs, like those of many of his fellow addicts, typically last for about three months:

> The relationship begins in a torrid whirl of enormous passion during which it's all flowers and chocolates. I mean it all and feel very happy and excited. But then something happens. I don't know what it is. I start feeling bored, irritated by her demands, which is ridiculous because by this time we have shared so much together. It's when she comes into my flat and knows where to hang her coat. The more comfortable she feels, the more uncomfortable I feel. And, in the end, I just want my freedom back.

Like sex addicts, those addicted to love are essentially lonely people, many of whom have been deprived of love during their childhood. This creates in them a need for love but *not* the belief that they are lovable, and the two together account for their addictive behaviour.

The following checklist, which I included in *Personal Secrets*, was compiled by researchers at Metropolitan State College in Denver, Colorado. People who have experienced three or four of the following behaviour characteristics or feelings may have a problem in this area:

1 **Denial**. Your family and friends tell you that you're involved in a destructive relationship, but you disagree with them.

2 **Immediacy**. You require frequent and urgent discussions with your lover in social or business situations.
3 **Loss of control**. You often feel powerless to control your feelings with regard to your love.
4 **Compulsion**. You've broken up 'for good' at least twice, yet you've always made up.
5 **Progression**. As time goes by, you suspect that your relationship is on a downward path.
6 **Withdrawal**. You become depressed and experience loss of sleep, altered eating habits, etc. when apart from your love.

Love addiction and sex addiction are surprisingly common, with estimates varying between 3 and 10 per cent of the population. In the United States both problems are recognized as serious psychological disorders, and a number of support groups offer help, the best known being Sexual Addicts Anonymous (SAA), Sexaholics Anonymous (SA), and Sex and Love Addicts Anonymous (SLAA), each of which models their treatment on the 12-step programme pioneered by Alcoholics Anonymous.

Sex addicts and some love addicts not only share distinctive behaviour patterns but also similar physical attributes. There are roughly equal numbers of male and female sex addicts, and of course many men fantasize about being picked up by a woman sex addict. In fact the experience would probably be less than pleasurable because such a woman only wants your body rather than you.

Because sex and love addicts are emotionally troubled there are often signs of this in their hands, most obviously in the little finger. As explained in Chapter 2, anyone who wears a ring or rings on one of their little fingers probably has sexual difficulties. Such people have problems with intimacy, which means that their close relationships tend to be fraught with tension and largely unsatisfactory.

The little fingers of both sex and love addicts will usually stand somewhat apart from the third fingers, and may even bend away from them or show some abnormal twist or kink. In fact there is often an accompanying inward bending of the index fingers, which signifies a selfish 'I want and I will' attitude. The lowest sections of all the fingers may be quite thick, so giving the fingers a tapered appearance, and reflecting the person's fleshy preoccupations.

More striking signs of emotional trouble are revealed by the palms. The anxiety caused by the addictive condition is typically mirrored by the large number of lines on the palm, giving it a 'fuzzy' appearance. The sex addict's heart line normally shows a pronounced upward bend towards either the gap between the index and the second finger or towards the second finger itself. The love addict's heart line, by contrast, will either be straight or will bend downwards towards the head line, both types revealing a more romantic and a less physical tendency than that of the sex addict. However, both types' hands are often marked with the so-called girdle of Venus (see Figure 33), which is typically a rather broken line curving across the upper mounts, about which one well-known palmist – Mrs St Hill – has written:

This line never allows its possessor to rest in his affections. It is provocative of over-sensitiveness and of jealousy in affairs of the heart, or perversity, of an excessive and exclusive mental attachment; although melancholia or hysteria should not be attributed to it, it makes the temperament difficult to live with. The owners of this sign are difficult to please, in their affections they easily misplace them, and are very unhappy in their love affairs, and should be careful in matrimony, they set their ideals so high.

Likewise, instead of the head line running straight out, or nearly straight out, into the palm, that of the sex addict and the love addict bends downwards, indicating an imaginative and impractical mental type, who finds it difficult to control his romantic or sexual impulses. The gap between the heart line and the head line is typically

Figure 33 Print of palm with girdle of Venus.

narrow, revealing an innate self-centredness and a lack of true generosity. The addict, in other words, takes from others, driven as he or she is by a desperate need for affection and attention.

Both sex addicts and love addicts often have tattoos, which are symbols of emotional disquiet, and the male addict of either type frequently wears a moustache, which can signify emotional and sexual inadequacy.

In facial analysis, the face is divided into three main regions. The Upper Zone or Heavenly Area covers the forehead, from the hairline to the eyebrows; the Middle Zone or Human Area extends from the eyebrows to the base of the nose, and thus includes the eyes and cheek-bones; and the Lower Zone or Earth Area is that part of the face lying beneath the nose.

The Upper Zone is thought to reveal our intelligence and mental type; the Middle Zone, our adaptability; and the Lower Zone, our energy. There should ideally be an equal balance between these three qualities of intelligence, adaptability and energy, and when there is, the three facial zones are roughly equal in height and width. If, by contrast, we have too much or too little of one of these primary life qualities, the corresponding facial zone will be proportionately larger or smaller.

The face of the sex addict (see figure 34) typically shows a Lower Zone, which is broader than the zones above. If partnered by a chin that juts forward, the two facial characteristics reveal an insistent urge to seduce, and thus dominate, women. The lips may also be unbalanced, the top being thinner than the bottom, a sign that betokens a strong need to be loved without the capacity to love in return.

Figure 34 The broad lower face typical of the sex addict.

The size and shape of our noses are also said to reflect our sexuality. A large, fleshy nose, for example, symbolizes a large penis *and* a strong libido; while a small, thin nose signifies the reverse. A nose that curves down towards the mouth signifies an insistent sex urge in a man or woman who is preoccupied with sensual pleasures. However, when the nose bridge is low and is accompanied by upturned nostrils – the classic snub nose – it symbolizes a general lack of direction and drive, loose morals and a dislike of responsibility.

Chapter 8

APHRODISIACS AND OTHER SEX ENHANCERS

APHRODISIACS

An aphrodisiac is any substance or drug that increases sexual desire, improves sexual performance, enhances sexual intensity, or even all three. Men usually take aphrodisiacs in the hope of making themselves better lovers, while giving them to women to make them more lustful. Many reputed aphrodisiacs are derived from plants, although most scientists believe that there is no such thing.

Whether or not aphrodisiacs appeal to you rather depends on how satisfied you are with the amount and quality of your lovemaking. When one partner wants less sex than the other, or feels their performance needs to be improved, they might try an aphrodisiac.

A survey conducted by *Woman* magazine in 1983 found that in England and Wales the average couple make love once or twice a week, whereas in Scotland they do so two or three times a week. The survey also discovered that only one in five women under the age of 35 made love more than three times a week, and that as many as four out of five women have difficulty in getting sexually aroused.

Of course we are normally most sexually driven in our late teens and early twenties, this being nature's way of maximizing the number of women who get pregnant when they are healthiest and most fertile. Thereafter our sex drive, and often performance, tend to decline. By middle age many people have little interest in sex, and may even have problems with impotence or frigidity. So it is during the middle years that people often start asking themselves whether aphrodisiacs might improve their sex lives.

If you are having any sort of sexual problem, you first need to rule out possible physical causes. For example, heavy drinking can cause impotence in men and a lack of sexual desire in women, and long-term use of drugs like marijuana, cocaine and heroin can result in a decrease or complete loss of libido. Cocaine, heroin and amphetamines can also make it difficult for men to ejaculate and prevent women from reaching orgasm.

Sexual difficulties are a side effect of over 200 drugs commonly prescribed for conditions such as obesity, depression, high blood pressure, anxiety, ulcers, heart burn, irritable colon and muscle spasms. Some of the drugs used to treat heart complaints and high blood pressure, in particular, have been shown to cause impotence in some men, while others weaken the libido, stop men from ejaculating, or prevent women from reaching orgasm. However, such negative reactions only affect a few patients and depend on the size of the dose, the length of time it is taken, and the patient's sensitivity to the particular drug used.

Certain diseases like diabetes and muscular dystrophy may cause impotence in men, while psychological factors such as stress, anxiety, anger and depression can both reduce the sex drive and cause impotence.

Eating a high-fat diet may also cause impotence in men, as the fat deposited in the blood vessels of the penis (a condition known as penile angina) eventually blocks them and so stops the penis from becoming erect. So men who want to preserve the health of their hearts and the potency of their penises, should switch to a low-fat diet. This means reducing, or cutting out, their intake of fatty cheeses, fatty meats, cream, whole milk, fried foods, egg yolks, butter, and processed foods made with palm oil or coconut oil. They should also eat more fruit and vegetables, fish, skinless chicken, lean meat and margarine. Because penile angina usually begins affecting a man's potency in his fifties, and cannot be reversed, it is important that he starts eating a low-fat diet while he is still young.

Certain prescription drugs, unlike those mentioned above, have an aphrodisiac effect on some people. For example, women taking the fertility drug bromocriptine mesylate have reported a heightened interest in sex, while men with abnormal levels of the hormone prolactin have also noticed an increase in their libido when taking the drug. However, bromocriptine mesylate has dangerous side effects and is now only given to women being treated for pituitary tumours.

But most of us are less interested in prescribed drugs than in aphrodisiac substances that are widely, and legally, available. As mentioned earlier, the Scottish apparently make love on average almost twice as often as the English and the Welsh. It seems that their stronger sex drive might be due to the fact that they eat more porridge than people living south of the border, if the findings of scientists at the Institute for Advanced Study of Human Sexuality are to be believed. They report that taking dried, powdered whole, green oat plants, extract of nettles and one or two other unnamed ingredients, mixed with water, fruit juice or tea, increases the sex drive, heightens sexual pleasure and cures impotence in men.

One very satisfied female volunteer who tested the mixture, said that she 'felt better, [had] more intense orgasms, and more sexual dreams', adding that she wanted 'to try larger doses for special occasions'! The dry compound, which is marketed in the US under the trade name Exsativa, is thought to work by raising the levels of the sex hormone testosterone in the blood.

What is most interesting about Exsativa is that one of the main ingredients is extract of nettles, as these generally disliked plants have been celebrated as aphrodisiacs for over 2,000 years. Indeed, in the *Art of Love* Ovid recommends that the lover should

Some pepper bruised with seeds of nettles join
And clary steep in bowls of mellow wine . . .

He also claims that fish spawn, white shallots, the root of the eryngo plant, and a mixture of fresh eggs, honey and the leaves of pine trees are all aphrodisiacs.

But while Ovid acknowledges that nettles – or, more specifically, nettle seeds – are aphrodisiacs, he does not specify which type of nettle he is talking about. He may mean our common stinging nettle (*Urtica dioica*) but it's more likely that he's referring to the seeds of the larger Roman nettle (*Urtica pilulifera*), famous for its potent sting. This plant is common in Italy but is only found in the eastern part of England.

Nettle seeds, however, are available from herbalists and can be mixed with pepper and soaked in wine, as Ovid suggests. Or you may prefer to take them by adding 1 heaped teaspoonful to some jam or honey. These seeds are said to cure impotence and boost the sex drive.

There are many species of eryngo, two of which grow wild in Britain. The sea eryngo (*Eryngium maritimum*) is commonly found in sandy coastal areas. It stands about a foot high, with stiff leaves and round, blue-coloured flowers, and it's probably this variety that poet Andrew Young (1807–1889) meant when he wrote:

I came on that blue-headed plant
That lovers ate to waken love,
Eryngo; but felt no want,
A lovesick swain, to eat thereof.

The field eryngo (*Eryngium campestra*) is common in southern Europe but rare in Britain, where it's apparently only found in an area near Plymouth and the ballast hills near Tyne. The roots of both eryngo plants are eaten to stimulate lust.

In another poem Ovid mentions two other aphrodisiacs, one well-known, the other not. He writes:

> Mushrooms of every sort provoke desire,
> Salacious rockets set your veins on fire.

The name 'rocket' is applied to several plants belonging to the Crucifer family, and it is difficult to know whether Ovid is referring to one of them, some of them, or all of them. For example there is the London rocket (*Sisymbrium Irio*), which is rare in Britain but common in Italy; the winter cress or yellow rocket (*Barbarea vulgaris*), which is widespread in both Britain and Italy; and the sweet rocket or Dame's rocket (*Hesperis matronalis*), which is a native plant in Italy but an introduced garden plant in Britain.

As certain rockets are also known as 'mustards', it is hardly surprising that they were, and are, considered to be hot stuff! This is perhaps why the Romans held the rocket sacred to Priapus, the lustful god of gardens and orchards.

Other reputed aphrodisiacs include parsnips, parsley, celery (best when made into a soup), asparagus, mint tea, nasturtium tea (made by infusing ½oz fresh nasturtium leaves in ½ pint boiling water), and the testicle-shaped tubers of orchids. One of the most effective species is the early purple orchid (*Orchis mascula* – literally 'manly testicle'), common in both Britain and Europe. The tubers must be eaten fresh and apparently work best when taken with goat's milk.

The fig has long been associated with love, chiefly because the inside of the fruit resembles the female genitals, as does the large fruit of the coco de mer or sea coconut (*Lodoicea maldivica*). Other exotic aphrodisiacs include the leaves of the myrtle tree (*Myrtus communis*), these being soaked in wine, which is then drunk; the stem of the African tree *Lissochilus arenarius*, sections of which are chewed like liquorice shoots; the roots of the American lady's slipper (*Cyripedium pubescens*), which are grated into wine and drunk; and the nutmeg.

Nutmeg is easily available and can be sprinkled on to warm milk. But don't take too much at once, as large quantities of nutmeg can cause hallucinations. Both mandrake root and the ginseng plant (*Panax* sp.) look very like a human figure and are said to have aphrodisiac properties. Ginseng is supposed to restore internal balance, thereby creating good health and enhancing the functioning of the whole body, including the sex organs. However not all ginseng species are equally effective and the benefits of taking it only become apparent after a while.

Until recently one of the most promising plant-derived aphrodisiacs was yohimbine hydrochloride, a drug extracted from the bark of an African tree called *Coryanthe yohimbe*. Yohimbine has been used for a number of years to liven up the sexual activities of stallions and bulls, and in experiments at Stanford University injections of the drug had a dramatic effect on the mating behaviour of rats and monkeys. But while yohimbine apparently does produce erections in the African tribesmen who chew the bark of *Coryanthe*, later research has not borne out the earlier claims made for it.

Several types of seafood are thought to be aphrodisiacs. Caviar and mussels are among the most potent, but the best-known is probably the oyster. Eat several raw for maximum effect. The love-stimulating properties of oysters have been known for centuries. Nowadays lovers might treat themselves to a romantic meal of oysters and champagne, preferably accompanied by soft lighting and satin sheets!

The most notorious aphrodisiac is Spanish fly or cantharides, the crushed dried remains of the blister beetle (*Cantharis vesicatoria*). This is extremely dangerous and should be avoided at all costs. It causes intense irritation in the urinary tract, and can result in kidney failure, convulsions, and sometimes even death.

The other well-known aphrodisiac of animal origin is powdered rhinoceros horn, whose claim to fame seems to be based on nothing more than the similarity between the horn and an erect penis. This has been a tragedy for the rhinoceros, which has been hunted to near extinction as a result.

Odour plays an important, if largely unrecognized, part in love and sex, although there are few substances that are inhaled specifically to provoke lust or to improve sexual performance. But it has recently been reported that the inhalation of – wait for it! – the scent of room deodorizers causes the blood vessels in the genitals to dilate, mimicking the effect of sexual excitement, so that they become congested with blood and ready for action. Breathing in the odour of liquid incense is said to have the same effect.

SEXUAL FANTASIES

We often use fantasies to excite passion during lovemaking. For example, a woman might imagine that she is being made love to by a handsome film star while actually being fondled by her unglamorous husband, and indeed the husband might make use of a similar fantasy to arouse him. Or we might fantasize while doing the washing up or sitting at an office desk.

These fantasies often fall into the 'I wonder what it would be like to . . .' category. The most common ones involve making love to a different partner, being forced to have sex, watching other people have sex, homosexual or lesbian encounters, and group sex.

Most fantasies – except those involving violence – are perfectly normal and may well enhance the pleasure of lovemaking if you and your partner decide to act them out, perhaps using special costumes or music.

EXERCISE

If you are suffering from a lack of interest in sex, you may find that you can give yourself some added zest by taking more exercise. In an interesting study carried out at the University of California at San Diego, 115 middle-aged men were put on an exercise programme for nine months. They worked out for an hour a day, five days a week, doing stretching and warm-up exercises, followed by up to 40 minutes of jogging or jumping on a trampoline. Meanwhile another group of men walked for an hour at a pace that did not increase their heart rate by more than 20 beats per minute.

During the nine months of the experiment each man kept a record of his sexual activity, noting how often he kissed, cuddled, and had sex with his wife or partner. Those men who jogged or worked out on the trampoline did become more sexually active, kissing and cuddling their wives more often and on average increasing their lovemaking from 2.29 times to 3.1 times a week. Their rate of extra-marital sex went up as well, from an average of once every five weeks to once every three and a half weeks. So the message is, if you want to boost your sex life, put your running shoes on!

ACUPRESSURE

If the idea of exercising doesn't appeal to you and if you doubt the value of taking aphrodisiacs (whose effects may be more psychological than physical), why not acupressure? This is a technique in which certain sensitive points of your body are massaged to bring about sexual improvements. These sensitive areas or pressure points can stimulate your body to produce sex hormones, heighten your sex drive, and possibly even enhance your sexual performance. It has even been claimed that acupressure can cure impotence in men and frigidity in women, although this may only be possible if these problems have a psychological, rather than a physical, cause.

The head is one zone to massage, the body the other. Begin by massaging the head points, then switch to the body points on the following day, and continue alternating on a daily basis. The various points need only be massaged for about ten minutes altogether. Do not expect immediate results – acupressure will take time to bring about positive changes in your sex life.

Massaging the Head
There are three pressure points on the ears themselves and one on the side of the head just in front of the mid-point of the ears (See Figure 35.)

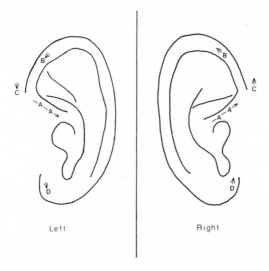

Figure 35 Pressure points of the ear.

Massage these points with the tip of your index fingers, using your thumbs where necessary, starting with point A, which is located on the *inside* of the helix flange of both ears. Massage upwards on the right ear and downwards on the left ear, to increase your body's output of sex hormones. Next, massage the outside of the helix at point B, again working upwards on the right ear and downwards on the left ear. This will improve the general functioning of your sex organs. Less important, but still beneficial, is massage applied to point C (which lies on the side of the head), and point D (located on the front of the ear lobes). These points should be massaged in the direction indicated, upwards for the right ear and down-wards for the left ear. The respective points on the ears can of course be massaged at the same time.

There are also sex-related pressure points along the edge of the jaw, and these should be massaged with the tips of the index and second fingers of both hands (see Figure 36). Start just below each ear, and rub the jaw edge with a circular movement, upwards and outwards, mov-ing the fingertips downwards until you reach a point below the eyes, from which you then work back to the area below the ears. Repeat three more times.

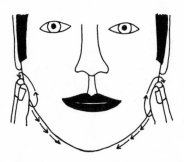

Figure 36 Pressure points of the jaw.

This massage action stimulates the ovaries and testes to produce more sex hormones and thereby increase your sex urge. It is also claimed to cure male impotence.

Massaging the Body
There are a number of sex-related pressure points on the body, two of which lie on the stomach. Other important points are on the spine, the wrists, the little fingers, and between the legs.

The main pressure point is called *ch'i-hai* (or the 'sea of potency') and is found about 1 inch below the navel. The second stomach point lies beneath it and is situated about 4 inches above the pubic bone (see Figure 37). Both should be massaged upwards, using as much pressure as possible.

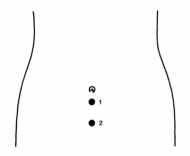

Figure 37 The two main pressure points of the stomach.

The third body point is situated on the lower region of the spine just above the hip bone. It should be massaged upwards. The second spine point lies at the base of the backbone just within the upper divide of the buttocks (see Figure 38). It should be massaged downwards.

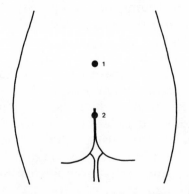

Figure 38 The two main pressure points of the lower spine.

The important wrist point is located on the inside of each wrist, about 1½ inches below the thumb (see Figure

39). Rub both alternately with the thumb of the other hand, using a circular motion, for about 30 seconds.

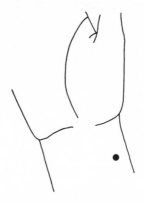

Figure 39 The pressure point of the wrists.

As I have already explained, the little fingers symbolize our sexual nature, so it is hardly surprising to find that they also have two sex-related pressure points.

The first is situated on the inside of the fingers in the centre of the bottom section (see Figure 40). Massage both in turn with the thumb of the opposite hand, using a circular motion and pressing quite hard. The right pressure point should be massaged in a clockwise direction, the left in an anti-clockwise direction. This action, like massage applied to the *ch'i-hai* point, will stimulate your sex drive and enhance your potency.

The second is found on the outside of the little fingers, just below the inner corner of the fingernail. Massage this likewise with the opposite thumb, rubbing across, towards the side of the hand (see Figure 40). This action will help break down any psychological barriers against the full enjoyment of sex.

The last pressure point lies just in front of the anus. In a woman, this would be midway between the vaginal opening and the anus. A steady pressure with one or two fingers should be applied here for about 30 seconds, to

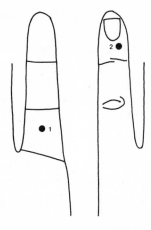

Figure 40 The pressure points of the little finger.

generally stimulate the genital area and the lowest psychic centre or *chakra*, which governs our sexual urges. If you find that the pressure causes a feeling of warmth in your lower body, this is a sign that your sexual organs are coming back to life.

It goes without saying that you need privacy to massage most of your body's pressure points, but there is no reason why you can't massage the wrist and little finger pressure points at other times.

SEX AND THE SUN

Finally, it seems that the answer to many people's sexual problems may simply be a lack of sunlight. Eskimo women apparently stop menstruating, and both Eskimo women and men lose their sex drive, during the long Arctic winter when it is continually dark, but they recover these functions in the spring and summer when the days are long. And it cannot be a coincidence that population growth is fastest in the tropics, where the days are long and the sun bright, despite the fact that many of the people living there are undernourished and in poor health.

Our sex drive is produced by the hormone testosterone, which is manufactured by the male testes and the female ovaries. This hormone may also play a part in our ability to respond sexually. So if a person's testosterone levels are low, or if the function of the hormone is somehow being blocked, they will have a low sex drive.

The outflow of testosterone from the testes and the ovaries is controlled by the pituitary gland at the base of the brain. Among the hormones it produces are LH, which stimulates testosterone production, and prolactin, whose function is unknown but which blocks the normal body response to testosterone if too much is released into the blood. So in their different ways these two hormones are vital to the body's sexual functioning.

The pituitary gland is influenced by the amount of sunlight that enters the eye. If we get too little light, its activity is disrupted, less LH is produced and more prolactin is released. This results in less sexual interest and weakened sexual performance, which is exactly what happens to the Eskimos during the Arctic winter.

However, it isn't the whole spectrum of sunlight which influences the pituitary gland – only the ultraviolet portion. And, significantly, it is the ultraviolet and infra-red rays that are filtered out by window glass. Because most people work inside, they effectively live in similar conditions to Eskimos in winter. The situation is even worse for those who wear spectacles or sunglasses, as the glass lenses stop the ultraviolet rays from the light entering the eyes.

So if your sex drive is low, perhaps all you need to do is spend more time outdoors, particularly on sunny days, without your glasses. Or if this is impossible owing to the nature of your job, you can buy what are known as full-spectrum light bulbs. Unlike ordinary light bulbs, these give out ultraviolet light, and can easily be fitted in your home or office.

If your sex drive and activity increased when you took that holiday on the Costa Brava, now you know it wasn't only the sangria that got you going . . . it was almost certainly that lovely Spanish sunshine. So brighten up your life by spending more time in the sun. And who knows, it might not be long before you're behaving like the rampant lover you used to be!

Chapter 9
TURNING ON THE CHARMS

The many sensual secrets revealed in the previous chapters should help you to find and successfully attract the right sort of admirer. But you may feel you need a little supernatural assistance to turn his or her affection for you into love, and perhaps even marriage.

There are many folk traditions on the subjects of love and marriage. Some of them may contain an element of truth but most of them are just for fun. For instance, a girl can supposedly find out her future husband's occupation by checking off the number of fruit stones on her plate after finishing a dessert of plums, prunes, cherries, or other such fruit. All she needs to do is check off each stone while repeating:

(Stone 1)	(2)	(3)	(4)	(5)	(6)	(7)	(8)
Tinker,	tailor,	soldier,	sailor,	rich man,	poor man,	beggar man,	thief.

The sequence is repeated if there are more than eight stones. The answer is given by the last stone and the occupation it stands for.

Similarly, to determine when her wedding day will be, she must check off the stones while repeating:

This year, next year, sometime, never.

To find out what her bridal gown will be made of, she asks:

Silk, satin, cotton, rags.

Her (rather unlikely!) mode of transport to the church can be discovered by repeating:

Coach, carriage, wheelbarrow, cart.

And the type of dwelling she will live in is identified by asking:

Big house, little house, pig sty, barn.

The unfortunate woman with seven stones will therefore supposedly marry a beggar man, will have no idea of when he'll take her to the altar, will wear a cotton dress, travel to the church in a wheelbarrow, and end up living in a pig sty! If she's sensible, she'll stay single.

More accurate information about such matters can perhaps be had on certain days of the year, notably 31 October or Hallowe'en, when the barriers between this world and the next are at their lowest and spiritual guidance is most easily obtained. Here are some methods you might like to try.

Go into your darkened bedroom alone with a lighted candle just before midnight on Hallowe'en and sit in front of your dressing table mirror. As midnight strikes, either comb your hair or eat an apple, or do both, and you will see, if you are lucky, a vision of your future spouse appear behind you in the mirror. Try not to scream if you do.

If you want to know the initial of your future spouse's name, take another apple and remove its peel in one continuous strip. Then throw the peel over your left shoulder with your right hand. The alphabet letter that the peel most resembles on landing is the initial of your husband (or wife)-to-be's Christian name.

His work can be determined by melting a small quantity of lead in a teaspoon and then dropping the molten metal into water, where – amid a lot of hissing and spitting – it will solidify into one or more hopefully recognizable shapes, resembling those of the tools he uses in his work.

To find out what your marriage will be like, get some friends to blindfold you and then line up three dishes on the table, one containing clean water, one holding dirty water, and one empty. They must lead you to the table and ask you to dip a finger into one of the dishes. If you dip it into the clean water a happy marriage is forecast, if into the dirty water a difficult and stormy marriage is likely, whereas if your finger lands in the empty dish you will supposedly not marry at all.

If you want to dream about your future lover on Hallowe'en, place your shoes together beside the bed in the form of a T before going to sleep, and repeat: 'Hoping this night my true love to see, I place my shoes in the form of a T'.

Another good night for doing this sort of thing is 20 January or St Agnes's Eve, which takes its name from the Christian martyr Agnes, who, upon consecrating her maidenhead to God, was put to death in Rome in 304 AD, when she was 12 or 13 years old. She is therefore the patron saint of virgins. You are supposed to fast during the day, then mix a small cake in the evening. You must remain silent while you do this, and then place the so-called 'Dumb cake' on an open fire to bake. If you are lucky you will see a vision of the man (or woman) you are to marry if you turn the cake as midnight strikes.

While fascinating and fun in themselves, these activities are only intended to tell you what the future holds. In themselves, they cannot improve your luck in love. For this you need to make a talisman.

A talisman is a drawn figure employing either numbers or words, or both, which is endowed with a magic force, capable of changing its maker's future for the better. Any love talisman must be drawn on a Friday, this being Aphrodite's or Venus's day, and must be written on green, unused (or virgin) heavy bond paper. Better still, it can be inscribed on a sheet of copper. Green is, of course, Venus's colour, and copper is her metal.

The first talisman you might like to try is made by

writing the following magic square, known as the magic square of Venus.

```
22 47 16 41 10 35  4
 5 23 43 17 42 11 29
30  6 24 49 18 36 10
13 31  7 25 43 19 37
38 14 32  1 24 44 20
21 39  8 33  2 27 45
40 15 40  9 34  3 26
```

Once made, the talisman must be carried in your shirt or blouse pocket, closest to your heart. It is said to attract love, give you joy, encourage harmony between a man and a woman, and make women fertile. However, it will only do so if you believe it can help you.

For best results a talisman, like any other charm, must be made when the moon is waxing (i.e. changing from new to full) and when the planet Venus is favourably situated in the sky, such as when it passes through one of the zodiac signs that it rules, namely Taurus or Libra, or when it is placed in Pisces, where it is exalted (see the chart below).

Venus's Most Helpful Positions for Making Talismans

Venus in Pisces:	14 March – 7 April 1992
	4 January – 2 February 1993
	13 February – 8 March 1994
	29 March – 22 April 1995
	16 January – 9 February 1996
Venus in Taurus:	2 May – 26 May 1992
	7 June – 6 July 1993
	2 April – 26 April 1994
	17 May – 10 June 1995
	7 March – 3 April 1996

Venus in Libra: 1 September – 25 September 1992
                             17 October – 9 November 1993
                             8 August – 7 September 1994
                             17 September – 10 October 1995
                             30 October – 23 November 1996

It is also helpful if Venus is receiving beneficial aspects
from Mars (which symbolizes young men) and/or Jupiter
(which symbolizes husbands). Such information can be
obtained from a good astrologer.

You can improve your chances of getting favourable
results by having one or more of the plants sacred to
Venus with you in the room where you make the talisman. These include the rose, vervain, myrtle, fennel and
the maidenhair fern. Venus-ruled scents like musk,
sandalwood, ambergris, myrtle, pink rose and benzoin
are also helpful.

Another excellent talisman for attracting love is shown
in Figure 41. Use a compass to draw the outer circle,
giving it a diameter of 3 inches, and afterwards thickening it by hand. Then copy out the linear diagram inside,
which is formed by combining the planetary symbol for

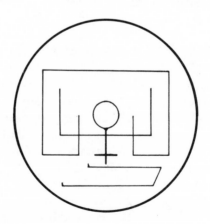

Figure 41 The Venus/Hagith talisman.

Venus with that of the Olympic spirit Hagith, the latter being a powerful force for attracting love. As you work, concentrate on what you hope to achieve, such as gaining the love of a particular person. You should also follow the guidelines mentioned above about the moon and planetary positions. When you have finished the drawing, cut the talisman out by trimming it neatly around the edge, and then put it safely in your breast pocket unfolded.

The talisman will need to be recharged once a day. Do this by taking it out of your pocket and placing it on a table at which you are seated. Again, concentrate on what you hope to achieve. This has the effect of willing your thoughts into the talisman and so energizing it. Concentrate in this way for a couple of minutes.

Another powerful talisman you can make has Jewish origins, employing the Hebrew word בשם, which means 'in the name of'. The completed talisman is shown in Figure 42. Start by drawing a circle with a diameter of 3 inches, and continue by copying the Hebrew word into it near the top. Underneath it write the word SHADDAI, which is one of the Hebrew names of God, or alternatively you can use one of the other divine Hebrew names like

Figure 42 The Hebrew love talisman.

Yah, Elohim, El, Adonai or Tzabaoth. Beneath that write ARGAMAN, which is the Romanized Hebrew mnemonic for the five angels, and underneath that write the English word LOVE, this being the emotion you wish to attract. Lastly, write the words AMEN SELAH beneath LOVE. Then cut out the talisman and on its reverse side draw the zodiac symbol for Venus.

The talisman should then also be placed in your breast pocket, where it will be ideally placed to bring about what you want to happen. But don't expect immediate results. Understand that both it and the other talismans may have to reorganize quite a few aspects of your life before they can make your wishes come true. So give them all a few days of work. This talisman will likewise need to be recharged once a day, following the procedure outlined above.

The talisman illustrated in Figure 43 is also worth trying, because it is said to cause love for you to grow in the heart of the desired person when you *show* it to him (or her). The Latin quotation it contains comes from Genesis I and reads *'Benedixitque ielis Deus et ait Crescite et muetipluamini et replete terrum'*.

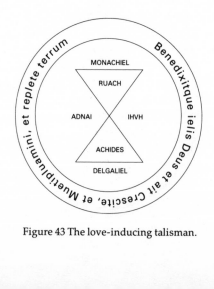

Figure 43 The love-inducing talisman.

You can encourage luck in love and good fortune generally by wearing one or other of the gemstones associated with your zodiac sign of birth. To work effectively it must come in contact with your skin, so it is most conveniently worn as a pendant, although the other alternative is an open-backed ring. The following is a list of all the gemstones linked with each of the zodiac signs:

Aries:	diamond, sapphire, ruby
Taurus:	emerald, lapis lazuli, moss agate
Gemini:	agate, opal, alexandrite, onyx, emerald
Cancer:	moonstone, turquoise, ruby, cornelian
Leo:	sardonyx, topaz, diamond
Virgo:	cornelian, sapphire, jade, chrysolite
Libra:	opal, aquamarine, chrysolite
Scorpio:	ruby, beryl, cornelian, malachite, topaz
Sagittarius:	sapphire, turquoise, ruby, malachite
Capricorn:	garnet, black opal, tourmaline
Aquarius:	amethyst, aquamarine, lapis lazuli
Pisces:	sapphire, bloodstone, coral

Most people wish to be married one day and will hopefully have their wish come true. In fact if you act on the advice given in this book, it may happen sooner than you think. But there are a number of lucky do's and don'ts to bear in mind on your wedding day if your marriage is to be a long and satisfying one.

The luckiest month in which to marry is June. This is because June is the sixth month of the year – six is the number of domestic happiness – and also because June takes its name from Juno, the Roman goddess of marriage.

The unluckiest month to marry, by contrast, is May ('Marry in May, you'll rue the day'). May takes its name from the minor goddess Maia, with whom Zeus (or Jupiter) had an affair, and has thus come to signify infidelity in marriage. Indeed, the number five – and May is the fifth month of the year – is linked with unfaithfulness and sexual promiscuity. So try to avoid getting married in May at all costs!

If you are female and virginal, you should get married in white, especially if you marry in church. However, if your name is Mary, it is considered both lucky and appropriate to wear blue. This is because Mary was the name of Jesus's mother, whose sacred colour is blue. It is of course both sacrilegious and unlucky to wear white if you are not a virgin. But all brides should wear:

Something old, something new
Something borrowed, something blue.

Many people nowadays marry in a registry office, which means that the bride has more choice when it comes to choosing what colour to wear. This is why it is important to note that certain colours are lucky and others unlucky, as recorded in the following rhyme:

Married in white, you have chosen all right.
Married in green, ashamed to be seen.
Married in grey, you will go far away.
Married in red, you will wish yourself dead.
Married in blue, he will never be true.
Married in yellow, ashamed of the fellow.
Married in black, comforts you'll lack.
Married in pink, your spirits will sink.
Married in brown, you'll live out of town.
Married in pearl, you'll live in a whirl.

When it comes to choosing the luckiest day of the week on which to hold your nuptials, the next rhyme will supposedly help you sort out the good days from the bad:

Monday for wealth,
Tuesday for health,
Wednesday the best day of all.
Thursday for crosses,
Friday for losses,
Saturday no luck at all.

So, for the best possible start to married life, it seems you should tie the knot on a Wednesday in June.

Yet even this will apparently be of no avail if you make the mistake of marrying a man whose surname begins with the same letter as your own:

Change the name, and not the letter, you'll change for worse and not for better.

Bad luck in marriage is also supposedly augured by doing any of the following things on your wedding day:

♥ Wearing pearls – they signify tears.
♥ Breaking anything – it means strife.
♥ Losing the heel of a shoe – it foretells trouble with your husband's relatives.
♥ Seeing the bridegroom before you meet him in church.
♥ Seeing a cat, a dog, a hare, a pig or a funeral while driving to church.
♥ Entering the church or your new home with your left foot.
♥ Leaving the church by a different door from the one you entered it by.
♥ Dropping the wedding ring before it is placed on your finger – this signifies misfortune.
♥ Keeping your orange blossom, if worn.
♥ Turning back for any reason once you have set off on your honeymoon.

But probably the best piece of traditional lore to take note of is: 'Marry in haste, repent at leisure'!

AFTERWORD

If being in love is indeed a form of madness, it is perhaps comforting to know that the agony and ecstasy are eventually replaced by more moderate emotions! The heart-stopping 'I'll die if I can't be with you' feelings seldom last for more than two years at the most. And companionship and mutual tenderness gradually take the place of passion and sensuous selfishness. For, while being in love is incredibly exciting at first, it is also a form of slavery, in which two people may become entirely dependent upon each other for their happiness. So it's not surprising to find that some people say being in love is the worst thing in the world.

Passionate love tends to last longer in certain circumstances. When the couple can see each other all the time, their passion fades fairly quickly, whereas if they are kept apart – by distance, for example, or parental disapproval – their feelings are likely to remain on the boil a lot longer. The disapproval of parents invariably strengthens the feelings of young lovers and thus has exactly the opposite effect to that which the parents intend. After all, it was partly their families' opposition that fanned the flames of passion between Romeo and Juliet.

The Greeks had a neat mythological explanation for the transition from grand passion to a calmer mutual affection. They said the first was caused by Eros (or Cupid), the second by his younger brother Anteros. The name Eros (from which we get words like 'erotic' and 'erogenous') means 'sexual passion' or 'lust', while Anteros means 'against lust', and refers to what we would now call mutual love and mutual tenderness. Anteros can therefore be regarded as the god of responsible, caring love.

And yet even when the feelings generated by Anteros are ruling their hearts, every couple has to cope with the day-to-day difficulties of life and with their own, often different, needs and desires. Why is it that some couples grow closer, while others grow apart – and may even separate and divorce?

I believe the answer lies in two aspects of our lives, one that cannot be changed to any significant degree, and one that can.

As I have already mentioned, happy couples are typically very similar, not only physically and mentally, but also in the benefits they derive from their union, whereas couples who drift apart with the passage of time tend to be unequally matched in these ways. These of course are things the two people can often do little to change.

However they can do a lot about the other important aspect – the way they handle the problems of life. According to research done by Professor John Wright of McGill University, Canada, unhappy couples tend to tackle problems in a negative way.

For example, a woman might say to her husband, 'I don't like you going to the pub', while the man might say to his wife, 'I don't like the way you dress'. Instead they should be emphasizing the positive. The wife could say, 'I love it when you stay home with me', and the husband might compliment his wife when she wears something he does like. The negative statements arise because both partners have got into the habit of blaming the other one for their problems. Such negative attitudes eventually destroy the relationship because they leave the other one not knowing how to please.

The second negative pattern, according to Professor Wright, is for one to say 'It's about time!' when the other does behave the way he or she wants: 'Here the major part of the message is, "I'm still angry at you because you took so long", instead of "I'm pleased you did it".'

By contrast, Wright's happy couples were all found to:

💜 Use praise more and punishment less.
💜 Use positive solutions more and negative solutions less.
💜 Be less likely to point a finger at the other and say, 'The solution lies with you, not me'.
💜 And be able to reach a compromise sooner than troubled couples.

Following this advice should mean that you and your chosen partner can look forward to many years of loving happiness. Of course, every relationship has its ups and downs, but good communication and a little understanding can usually help you find a solution. And remember . . . if the sparkle of romance starts to fade, a few sensual secrets should keep the flames of passion burning.

INDEX

By the same author:

HOW TO

READ

FACES

Our faces are the most versatile parts of our bodies, capable of an enormous variety of expressions. But the face displays a whole range of information other than just conscious communication — your character, your personality and your tendencies are permanently on show to the world.

How To Read Faces is a fascinating study of physiognomy, or face-reading, an ancient art of character analysis which Rodney Davies here brings right up to date. By following the simple guidelines and observing the illustrations, you will be able to interpret personality and fortunes not only from your own face but from those of friends, lovers, workmates, business contacts and complete strangers, their intentions laid bare for all to see!

Dealing with the seven principal face types and the significance of facial proportions and individual features, such as ears, eyes, noses and mouths, this book will enhance your ability to assess the true nature of those around you. Includes:

- the history of face-reading
- the importance of face shapes
- what your features reveal
- your face and your fortune

ISBN 0 85030 804 6   £5.99